2014

I0448005

Author Jay Kay

Published by
Jay Kay

vagabond!

Kris in his arduous journey of transforming villages in India, and Africa from the state of poverty to rehabilitation. From the state of frequent communal clashes, and addictions to the state of peace and prosperity by a Harvard Graduate from the United States!!!

vagabond!!!

© **Jay Kay 2014**
writerjaykay@gmail.com

writerjaykay@gmail.com

For "VM", Vethathiri Maharishi. Who keeps me awake!

To my family, friends & publishers with gratitute…

Thank you for all your patience and guidance…

Humanity!

The Universe has conspired,
Through you & me!
When the consciousness evolved,
In to human beings;

Animals are happy,
Neither do they hate,
Nor do they fight;
It is instinctive!

Only humans do,
Hence, the social setup;
To protect all to live together!

Born alone, &
We all will die alone!!!
Life is a passage.
Together we live (2);
Let us live in harmony!!!
By empowering every village in the World!!!

Prologue

JUNE 2020 INT. 5 A.M, NY, USA (Apartment):

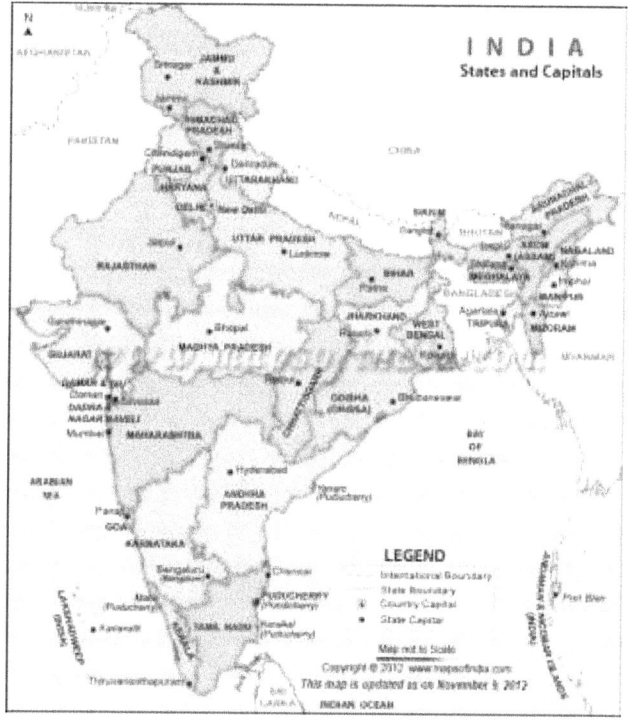

...India lives in her seven hundred thousand villages...
- Mahatma Gandhi

*V*andhe Madharam", "Vandhe Madharam" The ringing
tone calling for another freedom movement of this centu-
ry....'**Kris, wake up**' *it's me Sam on the other end, a*
nerd in the mid-thirties, and a Scientist was a bit restless
just lying on his couch in the condominium in the city of
New York.

It is a call from the Mr. President's office for the CNN
HERO celebrations. 'Mm mm...Let me catch some
sleep for few more minutes.'

"**Buddy, wake up.**" It is time to cherish as Sam
kept mauling him down in the cell phone.

"**What?** What are you talking about?"

"Mr. President wants to meet you"

I almost jumped out of my bed...I was still in pyjama,
searching for my spectacles.

"Is that a prank?"

"Oh..no, no, no buddy. It's real"

"I'd like to handover the invitation letter signed by the President." Replied Sam, my high school buddy.

"Of course true. The president of the United States would like to present you an award, followed by a Dinner at the white house. Your life will change forever.okay. Let's catch up to discuss the plans further."

"Okay. I'll be ready in about 10!" As I quickly refreshed myself after the short morning prayer, with a quick breakfast of rolls, French toast with a cup of coffee as served by the Doctor. Sanra. As the cat wags her tail in his bed 'meow' in the morning sun shine;

"Sanra...would you stop serving this please?" You are a doc. Above all chief of our hospital. Oh no. Mr. Kris will need the president of the world trust to keep himself healthy to look after millions of them...

"*Excuse me. Hello Sir.*" This is something, the lead and a scientist and the President of India has arrived in his regular attire with the sparkling eyes wanting to discover more in space.

Kris woke up a little late than usual due to the issues in the Organic farming, after carefully investigating the crops that have failed to produce and the drought conditions which has made the situations worse than ever. As he was reconciling his files to find out;

"I had a beautiful dream…where women and children are prosperous in the era of Golden times of India, where men were busy working in the field with the Elephant carts for plough their fields.
In the rice bowl of South. India, Tanjore supporting the World in feeding millions of people. The dreams were growing larger and larger and the vision in my mind was clear to help in empowering the communities that need the most, and my way was to start from the grass roots.

I looked at the positive aspects of life. There are lots of things in the West, which I admired like their belief in their dreams and seeking a continuous improvement in their quality of life. The East is a comparatively mature society with respect to spiritual thought process. Similarly, a large section of the population has a wide knowledge on various subjects."

The recent disasters in Uttaranchal with the Tsunami effects of extreme monsoon and floods affecting the Himalayan dreams of several youth, our lack of disaster recovery are apparent; these houses had been constructed with no proper plan or as per the basic rules have proved to be havoc. It is a disaster to the entire Nation, and the classical example of a failing democracy.

Sanra & I usually discuss Indian politics over a cup of coffee and breakfast, as she was bussy tossing boiled eggs with French toast. Sanra was brought up in the

US, hence she had a lot of questions about Indian democracy. She had the passion to serve the nation.

As Sanra interrupts;

Could you explain me about the India Panchayat Raj system? As Sanra asks:

"Sure. The Panchayati Raj system was implemented by British is a three-tier system in the state with elected bodies at the Village, Taluk and District levels." I added.

After a brief pause, she nodded. "Alright." She said sipping her morning coffee.

"Sanra, remember Panchayat Raj ensures greater participation of people and more effective implementation of rural development programs. The irony is that all of it is not working now; due to bureaucracy. Unfortunately there is a lot of work to empower these Panchayat Governance due to lack of good governance practices and supervising bodies, none of the plan gets implemented to support villagers, as a result the plight of children, and women continue even while India is termed as an IT corridor."

* * *

My Life in the US

New York, United States

The city of New York has the best sky scrapers and a well-planned city in the World. I managed projects as part of the IBM located in downtown, NY. I had an opportunity to manage large teams (30) as I shuttle between City of NY and Minneapolis, which remains my favorite place till date. It was an experience of project management and how tasks accomplished with proper planning and execution using tools, methods etc.

'Here you go Mr. Krishnan Gopalan ….the first glimpse of a young American lady pronouncing it a little differently'.

I interrupted her quickly …"I am Kris from India;"

My first day was filled with excitement to find the huge infrastructure, corporate buildings in the big beaver road, large grocery stores, and medical care. I was asked to fill out the Social Security Number application as I did and waited in the office. It was my turn, in few minutes the lady staff had asked few questions and then my SSN was ready. She said it would be mailed to me.

"Here you go. You are all set Kris. You would receive a mail in next couple of days." She reconfirmed.

I was playing back in my memory. A few years ago back home in India…

"Why do you need an International Driver License?"

"Sir. I am going to the United States. Is it so…where is your visa and the ticket? Sir…here it is:" as I showcase every single detail in the document.

The Inspector checks all relevant documents.

"Sare sare. Yellam sariya errukku! (Okay. Alright you've required documents!) Edhavathu donation kuduthuttu pooh thambi…(give some bribe bro)"

"What?" As was shocked? To whom should I donate and for what? I have all the documents, and my flight ticket etc. "Thambi. Listen! There are ways followed since the post Independent era. This is how our judicial system works. Just do it or get out of here without a license issued. You should pay couple of thousand rupees and move on, as I have other clients."

"Sir. Sir. I requested him many times." As I did not have that much money to pay him as I counted the bills…it was short of a thousand rupees and handed over whatever I had.

"Get out. I am not a Security Guard. okay. I will not forward your application to the Chief Inspector for the approval and license. Get lost." As he thrashed me out of the Government office. I was really lost in this event as I wanted every human right to

be followed and for a simple reason breaking rules is not acceptable in a great democracy like in India as I thought and left the place with resentment….

I was thinking about the Panchayat offices and the lack of governance practices back home. I believe the term village is a colonial term indicating the rural area. Every area in the United States wherever you go was well connected to the cities with the basic needs fulfilled anywhere in the United States.

This was amusing to me, when I compare the state of India with United States. There are few towns around that are serene, peaceful such as Salt Lake City, Utah which are well connected. One thing that I had observed was transparency in the US Governance. The awareness levels were quite high amongst the citizens of the country. No wonder US is termed as the best country in the World due to its robust Governance and policies that would reach individuals.

Further, I did analyze little bit about the constitution framework and what makes them stand apart from rest of the World: I had an opportunity to attend the Constitution class room sessions for couple of days to understand the American Constitution framework.

Harvard Business School

J ohanna was our instructor for the political science at the Harvard Business school…a tall blonde in her way of throwing candies for every answer was indeed motivational; as I had attended one of her special weekend classes. She was very passionate in teaching 'Political Science & American History'. She was discussing various facets of the American economy and the basic constitutional framework.

With close to thirty participants of various nationalities…I met her first the Indian girl sitting right next to me in the classroom was rather a quick introduction. A quick round of introduction, as I was interested in the just right next me whom I was attracted at the first sight…

"I am Gene studying political science, and the constitutional rights" as she said. It was my next turn, until she reminded…

"I am Kris. Studying computers and planning to start a social welfare organization..." as I heard everyone chuckled as the IT honcho starting a welfare organization?

"Interesting" as she said with wink of smiles around by the neighbor was feeling ecstatic;

"Dear Students, I am Johanna, lecturer for this session. I am going to walk you through the political science and the US constitution framework."

Kris as I called as in elsewhere...**"What is your question?"**

"Nothing. Just want to understand the governance..."

"Well. You would see by the end of the session"

As I often interrupted. "Who is the supreme power of the constitution framework" as she explained the 'Congress' which can turn the president down?"

I was the studious student of the class & Johanna was pleased with the blueprint project that I had submitted. I continued to work with her for several months to wrap up the blueprint project, which had a new democratic model encompassing the unification of boundaries, from empowering villages, towns, cities to connecting all Countries under one governance.

It was a sensational topic in the college about my project - 'The blueprint' project.

"This is so exciting." Johanna said and asked me to describe the blueprint plan.

I started off describing one by one. It took almost couple of hours to explain the nuances of the project.

"Dear Friends,
                    I had thought about this project for years now, after seeing the plight of poor people in countries such as India, Pakistan, Lanka and Africa. There is no dearth of knowledge, they will need to be empowered. They have enough wealth and resources. It is just that the wealth is not distributed."

I projected the presentation charts from my iPAD on the screen. It described how village can be monitored under the "Center scheme." It had steps to implement one by one to provide basic health care to all the facilities. Indeed, this is the first step to achieve self-sustainable model in every village, connected to the towns and metro cities. Our next step is to provide a united Governance model to consolidate boundaries of the countries. Each country is spending billions of dollars in the name of defense spending every year. Perhaps, if you can protect all these continents under one roof of the United Nation Peace keeping force, you can reduce considerably.

I opened up the forum for questions.

"I am a citizen of this country. How do we ensure all countries are secure?" John asked.

"Well. First step is to implement by continents. For example. There will be one united force from the United Nation securing the borders of Asia, then America, Africa etc. Perhaps, you can extend this after testing this model to two continents and one army for all borders from the UN."

"True…True"

"How do you intend connecting villages?" as Martha a student from Russia had asked.

"Well. That's interesting, Martha. Let me explain. Our strategy is to start a village, provide basic health care needs, education for children, and job for adults. Mostly, connect them to the towns and villages. Especially, in countries like India, and Africa, they all remain aloof. We have to ensure every government takes care of them, not as a political campaign."

Here is the "warehouse-cops" simulation software. It shows every district, taluk with number of household in the area. We evaluate minimum required no. of schools, colleges and hospitals based on the population. Moreover, the idea is to provide jobs by conducting necessary training programs. This software will capture data based on the inputs received from the 'panchayat' office every year. The software will help us assess the real situation and help where needed. Further it controls the government procurement process, and the expenditure to keep track of the villages. Your politicians will be given a KPI target to achieve, and they will be measured based on achieving the target. It will help us in preventing corruption in the system. The procurement and e-governance will become more transparent to every citizen in the World. Further, the warehouse-cops software will include alerts to protect women, they will get a RFID chip inserted in the mobile phones to raise an alarm. This will connect to the nearest police station. It is an integrated model, as it would connect hospitals to alert during emergency care, police stations etc."

I believe one of the key constraint is providing jobs for all. Our e-gov. model would map the skills to provide relevant opportunities to all citizens of the World, regardless of the boundaries. The skill match software will link the corporates to the potential employees. The salaries will be rationalized.

There are fundamental problems across the World in terms of sharing water resources. Our resource planning software would map based on Google satellite, to plan for integrating rivers globally. Moreso, in terms of carbon emissions to keep it in control anywhere in the World.

Someone in the classroom asked..."You have a lot of software..now, how do you plan to do a prototype" "good question. I have selected a small village in India as a prototype to start with…as Phase I, which is implementing the self -sustainable model"

This is great!!! As everyone exclaimed from the dean to all professors and one of the senators from Congress.

Johanna: Kris. Can you summarize the US constitution?

"If I understand correct the system is not just a one man army; instead it is primarily governed by the congress in the United States. The house and senate have prime responsibilities in the Federal Governance."

My neighbor was happy with my response.

"It is simple and a transparent framework with the President, Senate and the Supreme Court with Federal, State Governance of fifty states. The United States Congress is the legislative branch of the federal government. In simple terms state and federal are synonymous to the state and central in India. There are 435 representatives, each of whom represents a congressional district. There are two senators from every state (50) and the senate election is every two years. The House and Senate each have particular exclusive powers.

Further, I'd like expand the model globally using software controls for governance"

Johanna was happy with the response and had signed off my project.

The next morning, a local daily read:

"Kris, a *new kid on the block is challenging the Congress*"

As I thought, I'd like to compare the constitution of India and where do we lack in terms of Governance, and transparency. I believe our India constitution was framed with the base model of that of British model of parliamentary democracy. When the plans were concrete, however the sufferings of human beings brought the conditions in my mind, as I realized. It happened to me too...These are the points that I captured for better governance, looking at the robust procedures and the constitutional framework and lot of things to revise or perhaps amend in the Indian constitution for a better India as I thought by the end of the session. The class ended very shortly. I wanted to call her for dinner...but a little hesitant as I fear failures!

Gene and I were walking through the streets of Lancashire Park. It was around six in the evening where a car passing by intercepted and then pointed at us I was alarmed by the scene...I had observed a stranger looking at me for quiet sometime, and finally it happened as I suspected.

"Gene...heads down." as I pulled down to find my scalp scattered by an array of bullets from car as I cried for help.

"Help, HELP "as I cried to alert the cops on bike!!!

With a few police vehicle started alarming!!! The siren sound in the road of Big Beaver. Alerted the crime scene with a few roadside veterans witnessing the sequence of events.

At the police station:
Gene and I filed a complaint. Gene was still nervous. Don't panic. Calm down young lady...she was pale and needed an additional coat to keep herself warm. As I let her wear my coat!

"Mr. Kris...gives me your details."
"Officer, I do not have any clue." We were just passing by...as I stuttered still nervous realizing the danger to our lives.

"Well." The CIA interrupted. "Mr. Kris the intelligence agency had alerted me just now that they are trying to murder you...Just do the paper work. I'd start with the investations." As he wrapped up the filed while attending another case.

"Who. Officer?"
"Just hang in there. The CIA will find out!"

I was not even aware of the major story happening around me!

"For what...?"

"That's the mystery, to solve! It is funded by the con-gress!" I started extremely curious about the situa-tion, and worried about my life and Gene's. The puz-zle remained unresolved for some time. The next day Gene and I planned for a dinner.

"Gene, What is your plan for dinner."
"Nothing." as she winked away in the messenger, still wanted to forget the previous day's night mare.

"How about an Italian restaurant?"

"I love pasta and spaghetti" that was just right in time and good enough to find a nearby Italian res-taurant. It was a decent one playing some smooth Jazz as I look through her eyes of beauty.

"What are you looking at"...nothing, just finding myself in solace, as I felt like rediscovered self.

"Perhaps you talk a bit philosophical…"

"True, Whenever I feel within myself as she contin-ued from where I ended…"
Both chuckle…!

"What can I get you Sir?"

"Red Wine and spaghetti pasta with parmesan cheese & Red ster". ...PLEASE...

She loved good food at Casa Picolla. And then…
"Where are you heading up…" I asked.
"I am going North towards Big Beaver in Troy as I spoke…ok drop me on the way to the Louisville Carlton apartment to the west here." She replied checking in my patience.
"Interesting.." she chuckled.

"What do you mean?"

"Nope. Just listening to you speaks. I thought about our response. Were you serious the other night about the incident that shook us .What was all about?"

"Of course I am… "

"I heard it from CIA, It was due to the Blueprint, the project governance that I had submitted a week ago at the Harvard! Someone from the congress is trying to steal it from me."

"Oh My God!!!"

"So the enemy is within us!"

"Yes."

"Why would they do it?"

"They don't want us to implement anything good"

"Explain me" Gene asked, softly caressing her blonde her and checking the spectacles of blue eyes sparkling.

"Okay. Listen, if we implement this plan. US government will go bankrupt."

"Is it?"

"Yes."

"There is a lot of money spent on army."

"So..now, I understand. If you do this then the government cannot sell arms to the other developing countries."

"You got it baby!" as she winks her on the beautiful cheeks.

"Okay. Come on home sometime or perhaps to the orchard garden uptown tomorrow...will share the blueprint that I have prepared over last couple of years in college which started as a semester project which is my life time goal!!!"

It was a beautiful place with orchards near the woods park, as I spent my time over a weekend whenever I want to contemplate my goals, reading the vision of Swami Vivekananda. Whenever I crossed the Troy Union cemetery; I stopped for a while looking at each of those quiet ones, as the pigeon poking each of their hats of silent men around who had reached the peak of the corporate regime. As it implied me something, perhaps someone wants to hint at me by saying...

"Hey you look here for what you are? "

I pulled out my IPAD to showcase the prototype. She was glued like a high school student.

The real one, just face-off, It was summer; as the entire Michigan state was rejoicing warmth of the sun shine, as often we get a lot of snow, storm and cold weather most of the year; as I drove thinking deep in to my consciousness; a sudden experience!

"Where am I?"I envisioned a young man with confidence intruding me.

It's spring!

T he NEXT MORNING…A beautiful morning sun shine enthralled me with the scent of flowers in my garden. I woke up with the chirping birds.

Kris…"This is Gene…."

"Hi, Gene. Whatzup?"

"I've been thinking about what you said last night"

"About what." As I was still not in a mood for a serious conversation

"About your plans. Some blueprint for…."

"Okay, okay. Hang on. Don't talk loud." as I whispered. I will talk to you in the evening at orchards garden.

Orchard Garden

EXT. Evening at 4:00 PM EST

Gene…"This is a beautiful place, filled in with roses and apple trees. And children playing around peacefully with no worries of the future"

"Isn't it a heaven on Earth?" asked Gene.

"Of course. This is real heaven on EARTH." I emphasized it to her.

"Ok…what is the matter… about the success blueprint?"

"Alright. You seem to be very curious Gene…!"

"Yes. Because I am political science student studying American Constitution…"

"Sure will share it with you…but before that. Let me tell you something more interesting…."

I told Gene about my plans to visit India.

"Are you going to leave?" she asked soberly. I asked her join me for dinner in "Olive Garden", which is her favorite restaurant.

"Let's get some wine to relish our taste buds" as we both prepared to indulge in the most exotic food. I waited for her at the dinner table, which looked exquisite in a candle light.

I wanted the jocky to play the most romantic song of the night to impress her. She had arrived. A gorgeous, young lady in neatly pressed white shirt tucked in a dark skirt, which resembled appropriate English womanish. She looked absolutely impeccable.

The Chinese butler tried in an English accent…

"MaaHm - MaHy I take the o(ah)rder, please"

At Worchester College

I had studied bachelors in the Worchester college as you know…late in the evening, I was sitting right here in this orchard garden. A tall person with long hair, white beard in his white Indian attire of someone closer to my heart as I was trying to look through my mind for his name; couldn't see him though, as the fog was obstructing my vision. It was a Yogic experience.

"I am your angel as he replied. My dear friend what are you doing here in this country? I'll show you something…he continued, perhaps I have been trying to find you since you were there at a young age."

He continued talking and he sat right next to me. "You are deep in sober. What are you up to? Did you find the answers? My brothers and sisters are suffering. As I looked closer in his eyes filled in tears, perhaps tears of post war trauma, as I kept witnessing him."

I didn't understand the context, though I was patiently listened to the conversation. There were over thousands of them, men and women and children who were crying and seeking help. Some old men were diseased and the vision was through his eyes. And each of them was drowning in to a dark sea and I could feel and hear the voice seeking help…It's me, help me bro!" As he claimed some help from sufferings!

The vision had lasted for less than couple of minutes, but profound and left me in to a state for a while.

"Sir, I don't understand you? Who are you?" I was very inquisitive.

"You know me. You have been talking to me in the orchard, and back at the garden restaurant when you and I met second time."

It was a vision or dream or real as time in continuum cannot tell as I am looking for answers. It is reminiscent in my memories as I tried to recollect my instances of any such experiences of the past. Finally, he disappeared and never had a chance to meet him again.

These spiritual encounters are possible, if you are aligned to a subtle state of mind as I took the exit back home and parked my vehicle. Later I understood, It was a vision of Mahatma Gandhi as I realized after a while…

Gene: "Oh my God...how lucky you are? I just love it."

'Of course. I am' but Gene. I do not have money to do survive as I am dependent on my job for survival. Gene "It is true my life has been a journey. Evolving from the mundane to the revolution. Often times God finds someone to talk to and he chooses some messages to be passed on to you specifically couriered to you to drive beyond mundane plane of life.

'I hear that' as she walked away still thinking about his vision and experiences...we departed that evening thinking about each other and the visions...

A few days later...

"Let's meet Gene." As Gene shrugged her shoulders. Uh...I've got some work past 11 to find the community service center for a couple of interviews.

"What is that" as I asked.

"This is my project work! To identify the community service projects to revive the framework of services based on the problems identified." I showcase the CD and the project work book.

"Sounds interesting" as I nodded... 'I reckon there was a strong message delivered to you' as she nodded.

Often time you do not feel achieving something if you are endowed in routine tasks; until the day you find certain extraordinary experiences which happened to me. Gene continued interrupting me with all her questions, well..she is a perfect aspirant seeking a role in journalism.

"Are you contemplating on the messages you've heard in your heart?" she asked.

"Of course!!! Each of these messages could not have been delivered if I were not receptive. I contemplated in some aspects of humanity perhaps…to help the poorest and it was not a campaign in my mind, perhaps to give them an opportunity for young children.

I showed her the Blueprint for success to build communities that are self-sustainable model around the World to empower villages by fulfilling the needs for every human being in the World. The CIA agent had discovered that based on the intelligent report, the top congressmen wanted to avoid the blueprint……"The Blueprint" as I exclaimed…

"Why would Congress be against it?"

"If we do implement in a country such as India, it may well spread across Asia!"

"So what..that's for good!"

"I am afraid not. It is not good for the US!"

"Why"

"The exports will reduce."

"Which means?"

"Every country will be empowering villages and become absolutely self-sustainable."

"Secondly, US makes a huge money in large defense deals"

"Oh. I see the point now. So, If you're consolidating boundaries, US would lose its chunk of pie to the United Nation" as she nodded.

"Of course."

"What do you have in the blueprint?"

"Based on the research and the socio-economic reforms required…first a broader scope of one by respective Continents, Governance which is a little difficult implement"

"This is democracy"

"Yes. Perhaps, the real World democracy with ethical values in politics through the way of implementing a robust system of education & primary health care for all absolutely free of cost combined with the spiritual practices all levels in every part of the World."

"Kris, I love it"

"hope it works"

"Me too…"

"First priority is to start with a village and make it sustainable.."

"I should be travelling around the world as there is no different visa's required within continents!"

"Yes."

"We need approval from the congress to implement one governance or even ask for a sponsor from the US. Government, otherwise this project will become history"

"Perhaps, tough I guess." Gene exclaimed & looked at his eyes much closer. They had love in their eyes as they whispered the language of love.

***

Incredible summer in India!

A few years later....

Gene had returned back to India for a community programme post her graduation in the United States and connects again with Kris who was deeply rooted in several community programmes...

As Gene passes by with an address slip of Kris.

Do you know where Kris stays!

Yennanga? (What?)

It's about 5 kms from the railway station as the cycle-rickshaw puller said.
Ok let's go. She enjoyed the ride though she felt for another fellow being pulling the cycle rickshaw.

Indeed. A true ride of my life as she thought.

"Didn't get that?" I don't speak the local language. Krish Gopalan?

Oh. You mean Krishnan Gopalan...

"You go straight and turn right and then go behind the temple"

I reached up here as the directions were good enough after a 3 kms walk which I didn't anticipate.

Finally... she arrives in to the campus with small hospital, school for children, and few homes build of hut like and mud constructions which looked very neat and aligned with Nature with the reusable construction material used

Kris...as he walks out....

Oh my God. Gene. How come you are here?

Kris...as they hug gently looking at each other's eyes deeply rooted in the hearts.

"I am missing you so much Kris. I've decided to stay back with you;"

'Same here girl. As she laughs looking her shady shoes in mud. Chuckles' **"WELCOME TO IN-DIA;"**

Yenunga...interrupted by an old lady in farm outfit, who was prepared to work in the farm. Let me get in right there.

Gene...you relax for a while in my place... I'll be back at four.

Kris was back after a long day in the organic farm helping with improving the produce and training other adults and children in school.

Kris...I can't believe this...A school, hospital, several homes, and you teach.

Yes. This is my home! Is this your blueprint? I didn't realize that...

"What about me...?"

Gene. You can live here if you want? Without answering any further!

Gene 'I can't believe this would help me extend wings in every village in India, isn't? '

Did you know how many of them in India alone?

Over 700,000 of them and you have all the liberty to do so if you need one more life-time, will pray to God as I exclaimed!!!

There are about 53.1 million orphans in the sub-Saharan Africa alone. How are going to change the fate of every village

"You haven't changed a bit, Kris" as she looked intensely at Krish staring at him for a while;

"Thambi, sappad ready" (your lunch is ready) as I overheard with the giggling stomach feeling the sensations of hunger as interrupted by the cook to take care of my health. A long and nice plantain leaf, with the first servings of rice and sambar, with the tingling pickles and rasam. As I enjoyed the sumptuous meal, ending with the sweet payasam (deserts) I thoroughly enjoyed…

How many years did I miss this delicacies in the US with the fries and sandwich! Bewildered with the food presented which was yummy and delicious on what to eat first? A little taster and then decided to go for the rasam as soup and pappad as appetizers.

As Gene and I enjoyed a sumptuous lunch!!!!

As we continued in the next morning….I assembled in the World Community's next vision of Organic farm. How did you come up with this idea of the Organic farming…?

Gene…Look here is the Organic farm…I have the blueprint, which needs at least few weeks to explain. So I am taking step by step;

'Well. That's interesting' with an inspiring eyes looking at me, almost lock me in a trance of motions…*Perhaps is this, what they call it as love?* As I thought…and decided to hide my emotions…

Well. While I was in the US, I found Organic produce was common, and people had started funding these projects, due to the artifacts of deadly diseases such as Cancer linked to the pesticides used in the inorganic farming; which is our current farming all over in India.

Unarguably US government has banned in most of the villages in the US, however some companies have started exporting it to the Asian countries. This would result in deadly diseases, as I fear. Have you heard about GM seeds?

Gene: Oh my God. Never heard of that. What does GM indicate?

Gene, it indicates '**Genetically Modified**' when you change the genetically without knowing its harmful effects, it is like playing with Nature without knowing it.

"I hear that…"

To create awareness, I have simple and profound ways of Organic produce in our farms. This will earn regular income for the villagers with a plan to distribute vegetables through the society farm at a reasonable price, and it will extend to agriculture and dairy products

Hmmm...Interesting. Did you know in some countries they inject cattle, and they mix chemics to the cattle feed to increase milk production

I see. This is dangerous and I am not sure, what will happen to the future generations

Gene. Not to scare you indeed. To help you understand and the harmful effects of nuclear radiation...

Of course true. I have been hearing about the nuclear reactors of sub-standard material which is rather more dangerous to our country, especially with poor disaster recovery management

Kris is showing her excerpts of recent news, feature in a daily…

Look at the Tsunami, and a nuclear disaster in Japan. And they are planning to generate electricity with Wind mill operations; furthermore they would stop nuclear reactors in phases. The same is true in the US too, with elections campaign for clean environment.

Why are we buying the dumped goods from the overseas? Perhaps there is a political gain, who knows? Unless you get in to the electoral campaign

Why don't you get into the Panchayat elections?

Gene... Of course. I would like to contest as I can do more

Very good. Our country needs people like yourself who are visionary, young leaders who can empower youth and you have proved your abilities and I do not think anything else would be required beyond the sacrifices what you've done

Kris again "You are the best country-men...' 'I love you so much."

For the community service or me?

You will get that ...as she winks him away.

'Common Gene. Don't be formal. It is our responsibilities as I thought what have I done for the country except blaming someone for all the failures?'

'Gene has not changed a bit in become even simpler as I thought. Since the college years In fact spirited deeply rooted in his consciousness with a determination of a lion-heart to empower villages;'

One of Kris school friends meets him in the village... "Hi Jay"

Jay, Kris and Gene have coffee as they speak...a nicely brewed Java cuppa.

"Hi Buddy"

"By the way how is the IT market trend in India nowadays? "

'The competition is increasing; consulting opportunities with specialist skills are more as you have seen in the US. There is a lot of consulting opportunities here .I do see tons of students from Korea, Africa around studying IT, Business in Bangalore;' as Jay speaks through his dizzy spectacle.

"I feel honored to hear that…"

However. The stress levels has increased with number of diabetic youngsters is a common sight due to work related stress, and lack of spending time with the family.
"Oh no."

Gene, There were not more than top 10 IT companies in the 90's, and it has gradually increased with every top tier clients such as IBM, GE, Accenture, Cognizant, Cap Gemini, Philips, Vodafone and many more have operations extended to the shores of India.

I guess Delivery centers are doing well, employing thousands of young entrepreneurs, and engineers. It is a good sign of our economy providing jobs in the first place, though we should strive for product development, rather than the consulting services alone.

My only fear is that the economy should provide some equality without hiking up commodities which is creating an imbalance in the country between the top IT vs. non IT professionals.

If this trend continues, there will be a lot of vacancies in other departments, which is not a good sigh. We need to be balanced with appropriate tax structure with equal opportunities in every sector.

I have to opine. I was a Mechanical Engineer turned into the Information Technology consulting. Nevertheless now ended up in a different career. I was excited about the infrastructure, township planning and the down-town. Often wondered why we are far behind in achieving feats of success. Though, most of you would say it is because of population, what happened to Singapore which is more populated / SQ.KM with the entire size of country smaller than Karnataka.

Well. If it is possible for Singapore, India can also build up integrity and governance that can sustain. We need Government organizations, and MNC's to implement the best techniques in agriculture to help in organic farming. It depends on each of you, those who are dreaming about India a country which was once the Golden age where there was no evolution of Human in other parts of the world, India had the enlightened saints based of ardent inner engineering practices and discipline. I cherish the success of our inner world and the culmination of human consciousness has evolved, where east and west will join hands with each other.

The global economy will improve and the macro finances would be common as we are largely become dependent with goods and services shipped from India, China reaching the shores of the United States, and the authors. The actors of the western world becoming a household name in the East; There is a true statement that **'World has shrunk'.**

There is no point in thinking antagonistic about anyone or idealism, the conflicts in idealistic principles can be resolved through intellectual reasoning and science which can demystify everything with one common Religion and world governance. The basic needs of humanity are the same regardless of caste, creed and religion and it cannot be different as NATURE has bestowed each of with the same water to drink and food to eat. Perhaps the minds are conditioned and it thinks different, however the purpose of life is to reach the sublime and the ultimate consciousness.

You are born intelligent with success if you would listen to the language of heart, but conditioned by the society and various other factors thus attributing you for failure. The civilization evolved and has reached to the peak, first time our consciousness is evolving and it has to reach the peak to avert any mass destruction. The nuclear weapons have reached many countries, if someone uses it in an emotional state of Mind. It will be the end of the world!!! Let's build the universal brotherhood and realize the sacrifices and services rendered by great Mahatma's of the world. Your heart would melt in devotion.

I am not saying you should sacrifice for the welfare of the society. Just streamline yourself first, family and then help each other whichever way it is possible. The poverty is one of the basic problems in India due to uneven economics, and political in the World largest democracy daunted with plague called corruption.

Hence the Government schemes, policies are often drained perhaps, without reaching the poorest of the poor. As an end result it denies proper education for children who would continue with the same fate of their parents, and the sufferings never end
"Did you know the plight of farmers in India?"

There was a phase during the year <u>2005-2010,</u> where many farmers in Andhra Pradesh had committed suicide due to mounting debts, and it continued in several parts of the country due to drought conditions and inclement weather everywhere. India is a country of Agriculture, as our country men had the production of food, poultry and dairy products as the predominant industry from time immemorial. With the rapid Industrialization during pre-Independent India under the British Raj, and Globalization post the Indian Independence have changed the fate of India for good and bad.

The situation is that many MNC's have set up shores in India in the name of Globalization with offshore divisions sprouting out every year for utilizing the services, the basic needs of human in villages seem to be a distant dream, and there is a saying in Tamil language:

> *"The one who farm*
> *Is the one who has just a handful?"*

The basic economics should treat each of the citizens with inequality with a fair basic facilities provided for all. If a country is not able to provide fair economics, then the country is disparate in its economy and has no business in the world economy. It is a shame rather than claiming India's success stories.

I'd take you through the temples of Saranth, Gujarat to the centers of community services for her project work. They fly to the North and drive through roads to reach the temple of Saranath…How serene it looks with the architecture, pillars and its astounding as Gene exclaimed the surroundings of architectural excellence….I have all of this in my project for sure…The project World Community is going to win?

"Win. What?"

"Never mind." As she caress her hair and continue walking as I was soaked in her beauty of light green t-ee with a pajama which looked beautiful!

As Gene continued …
"Could you explain a bit about the chronicles of yogis…" as she points out to the pictures of Yogis of India

"India had a lot more to offer in ancient days. In the chronicles of Parahamsa Yogananda, and Sri.Baba you would find heritage of your own culture and the country. Instead of teaching the best of virtues, you seem to be denying it vehemently submerging yourself into the Western worlds. From time immemorial, India had these enlightened souls for centuries in Buddha, Sankara, Siddhas etc. These are the greatest souls of wisdom who have had the intelligence of Einstein with the only difference of theory vs. revelations, where they had the revelations of truth. The cosmic consciousness and it was natural to finding the truth in the evolution on human consciousness.

While our endeavor has extended beyond shores in touching frontiers of East and the West with the rapid Globalization shrinking the economy in the history of evolving human consciousness!!!"

"Gene, did you realize from time to time Nature is sending in its prophecies of truth in saviors of truth?"

"These are the truth cops who are rebellious to bring the metamorphosis in the human consciousness external or internal where the socio-economic factors are considered. In the form of Swami Vivekanda; who is an ardent seeker of Spirituality propagating wisdom of truth as 'Vedanta' with the first ever speech of a Hindu monk in Chicago which has its own significance. There have been number of revolutionary poetry by "Mahakavi" to create awareness amongst youth of the nation. Some of his poetries were ahead of his time…such as this and the freedom fighters of India…"

Gene; "Yeah! I have heard about a lot "

With the landscape and perfect climatic conditions, India can do Agriculture all around the year and suitable for Industrialization without impacting the schedule due to any extreme weather in most part of the India.

Nature has cast a play as it felt the pressure of human consciousness suffering as a savior Mahatma who had come to free India. In a similar term Kris has been transformed to a warrior of Kannur. An incredible warrior pre-Independence era of Indian independence' as she thought!

As Gene thought Kris was able to transform a village with over thousand households below the poverty line to a self-sustainable model in the history. The Government of India has not been able to provide basic necessities to every Indian as they look at the election campaign beyond humanity. This is a model that can set an example to UNESCO (UNO) to support in every country to empower the villages.

The rural empowerment was a concept of an emerging economy, and it is not required to relocate everyone to the cities.

Why that is every village is financially

backward as I traced the roots of villages to find a definite answer within self after investigating few villages in AP and TN, wherein the cities have expanded beyond the limits of IT corridor with poor infrastructure, funding to build the villages'

Kris continued 'Even today there are a lot of villages in India without proper hospitals, schools to support and jobs for adults. As a result, they live in absolute poverty and children with being educated turn out to be criminals of the future.'

As Mahatma opined…Today's Youth are the leaders of tomorrow!!! Isn't that required to build a country from the basic foundation of education for children those who are poor, and the destitute who need required care which is perhaps the principles of real democracy and the World largest democracy has failed to take care of the back bone of our country.

There is a rapid urbanization and people shifting their locations to the cities searching for jobs and the children are just the caretakers, and babysitters of the contemporary society. They are abused, tortured in the cities with the lowest pay and living condition to make the condition worse.

If a village suffers, a state will suffer and the country will suffer on a whole. If a country is inadequate to take care of the basic necessities of its people, there is no reason to feel proud of anything. Indeed it is a failed democracy and the state affairs are just a mockery despite being the largest Nation with several millions working all over the world. In a true sense, it is rather a shame than proud to honor the tricolor which has worsened the conditions post-Independence.

In every election campaign, there have been promises that were made of the upcoming roads, hospitals, schools and colleges and jobs for adults with ray of hopes for over a thousand household. This was never meant to be true as the calendar days reckon the hopes turning shadows of instances with no development whatsoever, and whosoever becomes the Prime Minister. **The situation of a small village, Kannur** remained in the political map of India with no further development.

The history of more than three decades of drought conditions have made the entire community weaker with no hopes of rehabilitation with the staggering number of people relocation from village to the nearby towns and cities for any kind of jobs;'

Back to the roots of Village

Before the aged men, and women of the retired farmlands have been looking agape facing up to the heaves and clouds to shower, year after year; The prayers of religious sentiments in the small temple in the village with the mother. Goddess listening to the state of affairs. Perhaps the call was made in heavens with Nature taking charge of the state of affairs, with the deafening words into ears of Politicians, hence the savior came in *"The Warrior;"*

The man on the field passionately named by the villagers, who had the humungous task of resolving the conflict in the region; in a small village in southern part of India;

Thus, a silent revolution had started in the village which has the blueprint of a success from the village of Kannur. It is just the beginning of a revolution, and the Nature's cast is now Globalizing the society in the peak of human consciousness.

One of the objectives of the World Community is to transcend beyond villages to empower the communities, from India to Africa. A contemporary IT Gandhi of our times, who is a legend with forsaken interests of selfless desires to empower every village in the World, and empower every community in the World!

While I was reading Mahatma's 'My Experiments of Truth' here is an IT Mahatma of our times, who has had very little interests of his self. With his desires of truth extending beyond the boundaries, and the wings of wisdom touching shores of everywhere communities are crying for help!!!

Gene thought…It is an intimate cast of mother. Nature in World Community, and Kris, who is an avatar of our times with the expanded consciousness extending his desires of eternity in empowering every community;

Every individual, especially youth are pride to carry the vote of thanks without identifying the electoral responsibilities. More so, those who are from the roots of villages are even shying away to name the background with a pride remark of an English accent with keys to driving Honda's which still remains the passion for a mundane mind. Whilst so, here is a gentleman who has sacrificed his well-being for the welfare of the society.

As our memories of US surfaced, we often visited the Benihana restaurant for lunch in the Big Beaver road…

It was always a warm welcome with the traditional Japanese shushi that I enjoyed to the core along with a few of my colleagues who loved Chinese, and Japanese food especially sizzling shrimp and red lobster with rice remains my favorite food till date.

Does that you fav. Food still…yes. Yummy?

"Of course." as she chuckled with her clasped hands and eyes locked with that of Kris, as Kris kissing her…

***

Vision 2020

The Next morning...

Hospital

Kris had been determined since the high school days to support the education of the poor, with a vision of swami. Vivekanda. He was a natural leader and the attributes of compassions. These days of wisdom have made him stronger with a lion heart to face and lead the world by his presence with a vision in his eyes, and words ceaselessly flowing through the mind as usual with his simple and profound etiquette of humanity touching several lives of thousands of the villagers…those who claim him as the '*Kaval Theivam*' meaning the Savior and the king **Kaval Theivam'** of the poorest of the poor and an Emperor of the wises ones.

Kris's ideals were different from others as he was holistic in his views as he spoke to me while we were in the US about the projects in a humble way…
I have chosen Kannur as my starting place due to it being my mother's home village; the knowledge of the people; the environment and the fertility of the land. My grandmother lives in the village and has about 3-4 acres of land.

There is also a huge home. If possible I will try to convince my grandmother and my maternal uncles to start managing the farm. If not, my 1 Lakh reserve will be used to buy and cultivate a small piece of land. My personal requirements are very minimal with a small place to live and the food from the farm. I will not keep a saving for myself, as I am against insurance of myself in this endeavor. The income from the farm should take care of my livelihood as well as some of the requirements for the project.

The determination of a teenager has gone deep in the consciousness as stated below. He was determined to marry a handicapped person…as some men in India should feel ashamed of seeking dowry for marrying a bride. What a shame. If you are young men? Think about it…Let's not defame the state of women please.

At one point in this endeavor he was advised by a retired Doctor who has wealth of experience in setting up the health care centers to limit the construction of hospital to a 2 bed hospital, which he had apparently denied as his vision was at least a 10 bed hospital to support over 3000 villagers in and around Kannur village, as emergencies cannot be always handled to Trichy hospitals and some of his childhood memories have forged his convictions.

***

Forged Convictions of Truth

I always had the real convictions to help poorest of the poor... My childhood is reminiscent in my-self...My pre-school years were mainly spent in my mother's village. And then high school in a nearby town, where I had to travel at least 10 kms every day. During this time, I was a carefree boy...playing cricket or chess. I did decently well in studies, coming within the top five in my class. Then, I did my higher secondary at BHEL School. This was the period where I started sharing and discussing my thoughts to give it concrete shape.

I contemplated on the business plan to start off from the grass roots to venture in to supporting human consciousness. If it is collecting a fund for the welfare of humanity, we do not know how it is being spent in projects, as I have my doubts in the governance of NGO's. I wanted to implement effective measures to change the way we think, a radical approach in holistic empowerment of humanity.

You cannot expect a poor man suffering from diseases, or dying out of hunger to grow spiritually. It has to start from fulfillment of basic needs as I have witnessed propriety in the United States where they tend to have a different problem. At least not the daunting problems of hunger and survival;
The basic needs are well taken care of in Social Security funds for all, with the food prices are at the lowest, and everyone could afford for a car as a default. I was even more astounded to find the sanitary engineers driving best vehicles. There aren't too many rag pickers as I talked to one of them. Gene reminded me on the vision that I've had a few years ago in the United States....

My Spiritual Encounters
New York, United States

I had intercepted an Old man on my way back from
work in Troy, finding him in extreme cold. Shivering.
Thought of helping him. It was a long winter with
beautifully decorate light amidst soft white snow
with children playing with the soft snow ball…and
few youngsters were skating wild adventurous to
watch under lights.

The ice-skaters were busy in the competition with MI Warriors vs. Chicago bulls. It was a match that my colleague wanted to watch for months.
I slowed down at lights turned to halt me. I paused my car music aloud in the Christina's songs.

I just peep out of the window as I opened my foggy power window of the Honda Civic sedan…Hi there…can you hear me?

Hi bud "Hi you there" An old man shivering in cold with torn coat which was not caring for winter... Isn't there a Christmas around the corner? And what are you doing here as mulled across picking up a fallible conversation, as I thought it is rather easier to start conversing with light minded person…who was looking to rest and dose off instantly;

I shook his hands a little more firmly. How do you do Sir? He was a little embarrassed for a stranger wishing him…

Well. I am fine. How long have you been here?

"I am Mr.Karamchand G;"

"Well Mr. Karamchand. I am Krish K" I introduced myself.

"Kris. How long have you been here?
It's about fifty years. He looked confident with sparkling eyes. Here is my coat. Just be comfortable. I can

offer you a ride. A little perturbed as he looked and responded: "I am fine Mr. Kris."

I took him to the nearest Café Day for a cup of coffee. "Mr. Kris. I have been living in this country for three decades now. This is what I have chosen!"

"Where are you originally from?" I asked.

"I am from South Africa. Haunted by the civil war and lost my family. I am just hanging in here. I was a business man...diamond business with billions of dollars earned; I had few diamond factors in the sub- urbs of Sierro Leone...which was all destroyed in a coup attempt and my family was confiscated; and with the support of my friends, I boarded the ship to New York." As he recalled his story of his life.

I looked his traces of sadness in his brown eyes and the nerves were string like showing his resentment towards someone...he continued...

"Well. I didn't want to work thought my friends had insisted me on starting up my diamond business. I had no reason. Nothing much except surviving! I be- lieve in God protecting me and there is a reason for my survival as I felt after several years in trauma. And then I had a dream...God talked to me. Of course it was him with the soft white light surround- ing and the path to the heaven was clearer than ever before and my sorrow just melted away like a snow melting in warmth of the sun shine. I felt deep cur- rent flowing in me...the love as I felt the warmth of

the eyes of my wife and my children and they were waiving their hands…'Be happy daddy'
As we are just fine and doing well up here in heaven and God was witnessing it all as they spoke up. I could hear the voice of my dear Sylva.

'Sylva, Sylva as I started crying'

'Papa. Don't cry. No cry papa' I am doing my home-work fine and don't need to worry as mom is here and God is near us. I am doing just fine papa…
My beloved Natasha was in tears…Honey, Indeed we are missing you…and the warmth of her smiles that I have not seen for years had come true as I hug her without letting her go!!! The clock was ticking as God has assigned time for everything it seems. Goodness God sent a stream of light to pick them up. Back home. I am again left alone as I cried deep out of my heart. God appeared to me once again and said:

"Man…You seem to be talking things very serious; just drop the body and be eternal. I will be with you ever if you have the heart filled in love;"

It was like words of Christ and a deep current of love healing me, my body mind and spirit. Just let it go as Time is a continuum and help others by taking this message…"

"I interrupted him..what was the message? "

He continued:

"# 1 Time is a continuum.

God – You are Internal! How would I get over my worries? Just remember you are eternal too
Is it so? You are eternal if you can understand time as a continuum.

2 – 'You are eternal!'

As the message was reverberating in myself "Time is a continuum" as I recalled my past as visions of past. It did look real though, but in time it just had passed away like a movie and God kept messaging me that I am truly eternal.

You should remain a witness as I will be with you forever. Your family is in heaven with me, so create a heaven around you and help others. It was like a prophet, a Christ indicating a message to me as I woke up next morning as I looked very young, at least a ten years younger."

As he signed and grinned for a cup of coffee...

"Karamchand, I could see your eyes sparkling like a bright sun shine as he looked at his eyes a little closely..." I asked him.

Ok, now you have heard couple of messages. What are you up to...?

Indeed. I pass on the message to you my dear friend;

"Is it so? Am I qualified to receive the message of an incredible messiah!"

"Ah! If I am Incredible, so you are!" came a crisp response.

"As much as I carry the wealth of consciousness; you do have it in yourself as he signed at my heart. Patting on my shoulders!!! Sen, My young man...where are you from?"

"Mmm...I am from India!"

"Well done. The land I'd call it as the spiritual host!"

"What would you do if earth is under attack by the aliens from space?"

"Of course I'd protect myself, family, and then whatever is possible to save the world." I responded to the question studiously.

"This is exactly what I was expecting Mr. Kris..."

"Well. The alien is not in the space, within us in the community which you will need to fight against. You will be discouraged in several steps as you would need to be courageous, brave and come what may as you would think;"

"'Do not stop. Until I hear the last child on earth stops crying;"

"Is that a message or a command?" I asked looking in to his sparkling eyes of wisdom.

"Of course, both!." And he chuckled.
"My friend, take this message with you and start at the grass root levels. Indeed you need the consciousness to grow, but without the physical well-being, mental well-being isn't possible."

These words were haunting me…am I qualified to receive the message and how I can ever build up something in people as we have too many organizations of spiritual context. How can I spread cross the message of Mr. Thompson!!!

"Kris…we have a project deadline as I was back to my desk on an upcoming IT Project with Ford. We have won a proposal few months ago with the first milestone was pending…My desk had been fascinated by loads of files, sticks with an embarrassing schedule."

"Well. Here is the plan;" as I discussed with the team with a challenge to deliver the project. I worked in Troy, MI in a software consulting firm; I drove early in the morning to work to start ahead of rest of all to remain abreast of the client requests. After six months of efforts with over sixteen hours a day including the weekends.my boss called me!

"Your team has done it very well... Congrats and I am going to forward your name for the leadership award." As my boss Mark in fifties, wearing a perfect blue suit said. Indeed, a nice boss!

"Thanks Mark. I'd rather request you for a team award." I responded.

"That's the spirit young man ..." as he walked the talk to award the team in few weeks. The entire team was jubilant with the songs, and partying the whole week as I remained calm to make an announcement.

"Friends, I have an important announcement. I mean. Today is my last day at work. What? As the team asked in chorus. Yes. I am moving back to India, Trichy my hometown. I've missed a lot in these five years of my work though I enjoyed every moment of my work in the US. I would like to thank this Nation for providing opportunities to excel and spot the right talent, and nurture them. However, my thought is not to settle for some wealth. I derive my deepest sense of satisfaction with responsibilities in taking back key messages of Mr. Thompson...that had transformed my life for good reasons. I am committed to helping the society, and serve the poor in every part of the World through an enterprise model. I would like to start with my Country first, and extend beyond the shores of Africa where Mr. Thompson is originally from! & I'll start from the grass roots of providing the basic needs for all."

I continued with the glued audience, who cannot digest what was going on in the party, listening to my speech.

"I had found my roots of consciousness; just want to hold on to it and sail where it takes me." The atmosphere changed as each one of us, including myself was speechless. As I asked. .but Sen... You could do it from here, US right?

Gene…. "No it is not possible as I have to start at the grass roots of Governance. A lot more to do and monitor inch by inch every possible workout that I have to. And the leadership skills that I have developed in recent times, Technology that I have learnt' is all required for me to support the poor and young children to being with…"

"Ok. I appreciate your step forward and we wish you all success in your endeavors and we promise to support you in the challenges ahead and road map was not easy!"

The entire team congratulated me once again and the thank you note was phenomenal, leaving my heart warmer than ever as I looked through my itinerary.
I spent almost six months in blueprint at the grass root level with finally shortlisted Kannur village for resolving the conflict that I've observed over months.

After six months of deliberate attempts to consolidate my finances and after I sold my Honda SRV..there was fair bit of balance in my account to invest back home. I booked the tickets to India.

First, I had spent few months in Chennai to register the enterprise and then shortlisted a village that I was closer to from my childhood. A village that had been tormented by the sequences of extreme draught conditions and the plight of poor farmers who were debt ridden and some of them had committed suicide. In addition, there were communal clashes every now & then. The news haunted me.

I just educated them...

"Yempa.why do you fight with each other? I asked one of the youth leader to refrain from provoking communal clashes. "We are one and the same." I said. "They are all your brothers regardless of caste and creed or Religion. Did you know you are all made of the same stuff?" I continued.

"Ahda poonga sir (you go)"...he responded. "We are fighting because we get paid for the clashes at times and fed a plat meal and wild rum;" "What?" As I was shocked to hear that and based on my enquiry found there have been number of political wings rooted in the clashes for no reasons at all.

I ran from the pillar to the pole for the NGO setup with the lack of basic infrastructure. First I decided to build a home for myself and a few poor people. At least ten homes to support the impoverished. I looked at the bricks making and studied a simple and profound technique to make bricks, as we did brick by brick with some masonry to build a nice home.

I had architected the homes for each of the family. A simple home which is neat and clean with enough space for a family. By the time, collector has approved my orders. Needless to state the relentless walks and cycling to the collector office to demonstrate the pitiable living conditions of the community.

I show cased one of the children who had died in diarrhea and another one who was malnourished with relevant facts of at least ten families whom I had surveyed in less than couple of months. With the support of my friends, and my capital was good enough to start the constructions.

After day and night of couple of months, my home was ready…as I walked in with a determination to build a hospital with the image of 'Ambuja' reminding me several times about the venture.

I asked the collector for the approval at the center of the village 'Kannur', at the North East where most of them work and live. To make it affordable in terms of facilities and commute. Often time's success comes in after arduous journey through the Sahara deserts; It was very hard with the Organic farming not yielding the produce and the agriculture was down due to the extreme draught conditions…there was no good news!

*"Uncle. Uncle"*as the girl child Sheila was crying for his attention. Uncle is busy. "Tell me as I tried to avoid her…." embedded deep in my laptop!

"Uncle. I have passed in I STD in rank # 1." as her eyes gleamed and her mother dedicated Vijaya's support in his endeavor:

"Sami... Yenga pollanga padikanumnoo pad- upadareenga...Neenga nalla eruko- num...vunga vamsam nalla erukkomnum. Neenga 100 year's vazhanum ayya" with her tears foaming in her eyes;

"You're my God....All our children are studying well because of you...May God bless you with long & healthy life over 100 years!"

"Sir. It is because of your efforts that our children who are impoverished are able to study well." I was determined to make each of them an Engineer, Doctor as a learned men and women."

"We wish you live over hundred years, and your family to live in prosperity. May God wish you all good health? Prosperity and happiness" as I stood speechless, looking at the group of men & women in a simple Indian attire wishing me all goodness.
In that moment, I realized my entire career of just working for money and passion for projects faded a million miles away and all my success have gone deep under rubble. Isn't this Love and sacrifices and the joy that I felt in the current of love was astounding and it touched my heart as well.

I was comfortable in a simple attire of dhoti and a cotton shirt and responded in a humble tone:

"Amma. I just did my duty" & I was engrossd in day to day activity and he was not getting in to the political debate in any of the occasions that I have witnessed as his approach was like Swami Vivekananda...and the student loves him a lot for his ardent skills in teaching computers to the children.

"Inga parungal Uncle as someone interrupted me by saying...*Enjarunga (look) 'paint brush la painting panniten.*"

She was smiling, seeing her digital prints of Kodak moments of wisdom...As I was touched by the angels of wisdom wanting to tell me something and the under current flow in my heart was astounding and each day passed by with sequences of life transforming events. I started enjoying the small hut, a sumptuous lunch and a modest dinner in Rhagi roti and the early morning porridge with children around me, brought in memories of my past childhood.

I could see my search for happiness in each of these eyes of children, and the smiles of men and women as they enjoyed the harvest festival of 'Sankaranti' as a token of appreciation of cattle, labors and the Sun GOD who has helped in a good harvest. KRIS was there with the pot filled in rice from the farm and he lighted after praying something to the SUN GOD.

When I enquired he said...."I am saying thank God for another morning with your grace filling my inner self with courage to continue till the extent possible."

The village atmosphere was very intense with the ladies had started singing, and children dancing everywhere with a bon-fire. And the old men and women were busy preparing side dishes to serve the rest of the people around there. The plantain leaves were ready to serve. It was a good lunch with sweet pongal (made of steam rice and jiggery watching television and someone busy enquiring about the homework for the day!

"Do you ever sleep?" As Gene asked

Kris…with a little smile. If I sleep, who would take care of these children as he sighed teaching basic grammar to a child in the IST grade?

"Past – Presence and Future tenses…." Did you get it? As she nodded her head busy preparing for upcoming tests conducted in the school…

"Anna (bro), Anna talk to my friend" who is

addicted to alcohol…he walks in, with the student cum addicted host. And asks him the reason, first he never said no to it. He was rather confronting the situation to identify the real self in the person, almost after an hour of counseling, the person seem to have agreed to get over his addictions.

I had offered him to work in his farm for next 30 days and the prescription of an alternate sweet curd prepared for him every morning. I rang up the adolescent kid after couple of months to find his scores have improved and his parents thanked me for the support in counseling the child.

"Sir…". As Mari said with tears rolling down.

"I feel happy now, since you listened to me and my weaknesses patiently offered me help for no reason at all and I was touched by your love. Which was like a mother advising her child? I will be there for you till my life time Saar in every step you take." Mari is a strong young man with a circle of influence in his terms. Who kept weeping for a while…

"Azhathada thambi (don't cry)…just look at me. I am your brother. We should help each other da!" I patted him on his shoulders. It is good to come back.

"Thambi vudayan padaikoo anjan"

"The one who has brother is not afraid of any wars" as the saying goes. He had washed his tears away…I had insisted him to go-ahead with the duty and continue in his studies and work in the field.

"I need your support in the organic field…" I asked.

"Okay, Thalaiva (Guru). I will be there for you at any time." as he whispered in his ears and started walking in his folded lungi and Hawaii chap pal calling Kris as the savior *'Yenga Vooru Kavakaroo'.*

***

Health for All!

Gene and I inaugurated the village Hospital
...and the World community was born with a broad banner stating:

'WORLD COMMUNITY RURAL EMPOWERMENT FOUNDATION'

I love it...as she found a comfortable chair at the hospital.

Kannur is a typical caste-based village in Karnataka where agriculture is the most important occupation. As it is, Kannur lies on the southern border of these two districts which in turn poses its own set of administrative challenges? Some of the administrative departments come under the jurisdiction of Perambalur and some Other with Karnataka.

Kannur has a population of about 10,000 belonging to some 13 different castes and at least 2 different religions –Hindu and Islam, predominantly the former. There is a clear area demarcation for the Schedule Caste and the Schedule Tribe community.

Gene…look at the crowd there …each of them loves me!!!

The whole crowd was cheering at Kris…Gene hugged him to stay closer to him. It was an emotional transcription of love that has blossomed without even pronouncing it...which was not required anyways as it looked obvious?

Kris reminds Gene about the challenges in procuring the site…
Kris…Sir. We need have identified a larger site adjacent to your site for the village empowerment office'
Veluchamy 'I do not care'

It is hard to crack the nuts as I thought after a heated argument between the villagers and the land owner…

This is my land and I will not sell it to anyone…and he left

At times Nature wants us to wait, perhaps indefinitely as the project was delayed without being able to procure this land which was right in the middle of the proposed plan for the World Community office, hospital and school.

'Oh my God…' as I gasped with my open arms facing the skies. If at all, I could fly. Would go to heavens to yell at
God who has created us!

 A few months later…Veluchamy came forward

'Thambi…Neenga yennudaya landa eduthukonga' take my land!!!

I was calculating a price in my mind. How much as I asked

'Thambi. Oru paisa venam'

I didn't know the reason as I went back. Perhaps God would have heard my prayers…as I thanked him!

After a week later Preeti indicated it me

"Avunga ponnu 'Rajamani' is suffering from Tuberclosis….who….." (His daughter is suffering from TB)

Who is that girl who?

Do you remember the lean girl who was approaching us for an emergency medication, admitted at our temporary van?

Oh my God. Of course I do remember!

She is the one…OMG!!!

What a game that Nature has played as I thought….all is set and move on to the required.

"Team – Get start go." Now find the ways to procure required materials for construction. As Kris started his army of young men, and women.

Here is the blueprint. I will consult an Engineer to form the layout.

Ok Sir.

The team after completing the morning breakfast of kepankoozh (porridge) and a banana with the strength of thousand elephants, they marched along with the master following his trails of wisdom

Here are the proposed homes for ten of them. My home in the center. No power is required for me, as I will manage, ensure we have the French window here…and the arch and the open window to discuss with the public. A greeting hall to meet the village leaders. Etc.

There was no prayer hall. Sir?

My entire house is a prayer hall, and my villagers are the messengers of God as he walked away looking at the 10 bed hospital plan

Here is the emergency ward…by the time in dusk he moved back to the temporary abode. With a few still discussing his plans!

After a light supper…of a cup of rice, dhal and roti. He dosed off!

What an incredible messenger as I witnessed him working dawn to dusk, as I moved back in project work just thinking as a futile efforts to managing the project work, which was not getting anywhere!

Next, going to the document writer's office to pay the fees, the team was shocked to learn that his charges Included the bribes for the Sub-Registrar - an understanding worked out by that officer to evade anticorruption raids.

The team tried to make sense with the office and could have fought till the end, but decided not to, considering that Mr. Sethuratnam, a senior citizen who is already dejected with the wane of the system, would have been pulled through the entire accompanying muddle. The first major challenge at the village turned out to be a beautiful experience, confirming our belief in the existence of well-developed village civic system. The proposed path from the main road to the project site runs on the banks of the public storm drain. Normally in the village, the land owner, in this case our farm's neighbor – a resident of Sri Lanka, adjacent to such public lands claims ascertain area of the bund as an acceptable encroachment by way of maintaining the drain.

Although we had the council's as well the majority of the village people's consent to lay the path, we decided to also have the neighbor's favorable consent.

The only say the World Community team had during the meeting was that the neighbor should either give his consent free of cost as his part to the whole effort or our settlement cost was non-negotiable. The choreographing was so perfect that during the actual meeting the neighbor's conscience was completely kindled and he could take no other position than to settle the issue free of cost with a happy mind!

He even took us out for a dinner and has lately been very interested and supportive in our works! Kannur is a dry land area dependent entirely on rains for water. The past few years of drought and incessant drilling of bore and tube wells has meant that the water table has gone well below 200 feet in many places. The current well in the farm has only sufficient water to irrigate about 60% of the farm. So, we decided to drill a bore after due geological testing. Even after drilling 260 ft., the bore did not yield water which meant a good amount of money down the drain. By June end, the well had just 5 ft. water.

We had also started the foundation digging activity of the hospital blocks and were quite concerned on proceeding further on the construction activity.

In the interim the architectural design and plan were done with the help of volunteer civil engineers and architects. Architectural design reflects rural life - is simple but practical and appealing.

Most material used in the construction is low cost and environment friendly like earthen bricks, earthen tiles and thatching. Most of material for construction was locally sourced - An all-women's unit took up the brick making, using hand press machines, during course of construction.

Most of the labor for the construction came from the village. Has helped establish trust among the villagers about the mission of World Community and role they can play in their own development

the construction of reading room too has been successfully completed along similar lines to the health center. The major objective of the reading room is to provide an informal education to children of the village (4 - 14) yrs. Emphasis is on imparting useful real life education which the children can relate to and put to quick use.

For the children between 4 -9 yrs. the main subjects would be Tamil and mathematics. In addition to the above the room will also serve a small library - providing newspapers, magazines and books.

A week after meeting the officials, Kannur experienced such a rainfall not seen in the past 10 years. All the storage tanks overflowed and our own farm was under a foot of water. In less than a week the farm well rose by 25 feet!

Along with this, the dug foundations caved in. Even though this meant re-work, all worries for water were also washed away for the entire year. With more rains on the forecast;

World Community team decided to push at a faster pace the foundation work even if it meant jumping the law by using the existing agricultural water source for construction activity. We do not have an easy solution with respect to electrical power, unless we decide to give into the officials which would mean a substantial recurring expense. With our current setup, there is likelihood that the officials will harass the team by sending audit squads, but we have decided to take it head-on.

This to "power" overcome challenge, the World Community team has made a conscious decision to harness the solar power for our entire electrification. A project proposal is on the works and will be sent to you in a week's time for your perusal. Our working team has been growing in the past few months as the construction activity is getting heated up.

The number of volunteers, branches, Friends of World Community is ever increasing, and the network of wellwishers worldwide is overall a lakh from every corner of the world and the number is ever increased year over year.

Lead the World!

*"**Left, Right. March**"*…as Kris, the leader of contemporary India was leading the march past. With the ardent leadership of an IT giant who is in simple attire of Gandhian dhoti was walking along his way leading thousands of children with the Morning Prayer.

With the network of several all NGO's following his footpath in transforming villages, and the social media is extending Vijaya's vision beyond shores from South Arcot to SFO.

Each of these children are taught to meditate, practice simple techniques of breathing to form a community of mental and physical strength.

Each of these children would become a Scientist, Teacher, Professor, Social Activist, Engineer, Doctor, and Artist. Above all, they would also transform as an Individual and a good human in evolving consciousness.

They would expand the vision of World Community to the world across boundaries with no barriers or anything whatsoever, where the consciousness is where the World Community team would belong, and not restricted by the man-made boundaries or layers of mind.

Gene 'I will be there in a minute; training few students for the upcoming Independence Day celebrations. When I was studying in my native village, there were few instances that I had witnessed. It is in my conscious mind as the cry of the mother is still there deeper in my heart!

Early in the morning as the rooster Cooing - cockaracoo…as it is a little perturbed for some reason. My grand-mom takes care of pregnant women, as in those days there were very few hospitals. My village was not an exception, as we need to go to a hospital almost 30-40 kms away from the village by crossing the local village roads which takes hours to pass by

"Is someone there…Ambuja ma is suffering from extreme pain. Can you help her?"

My grand mom woke immediately, and started walking towards the balcony to sigh that she will be there in a minute. She was there and there was a complication in the childbirth as the mother was crying louder for help. My grand mom had arranged for the bullock cart to support to take her to the nearby hospital

"Ambuja. Just stay calm." We will take you to the nearest hospital in town. Just hang in there...as she kept talking to her to keep her conscious to avoid any further complications. About 10 kms downs the trail, wheel of the bullock cart fell into a pit, and it was difficult to raise the wheels. Mari who was riding the cart had to jump as he tried to life the wheels, which didn't help and called for help...

"Anyone there" please helps us as he frantically cried for help. Where there wasn't anyone!

"Bah bah ......go. Get the hell out of here" as he kicked the bulls to try...finally, after his arduous attempt for half an hour, he was able to get it back on track and the bullock cart started moving at a reasonable speed..By now, Ambuja was almost fainting. Ambuja, Ambuja listen to me as my grand-mom kept sprinkling water in her face to keep her awake! Finally it took almost couple of hours reaching the hospital in town, didn't realize that there would other challenges.

My grandmother and Mari carried Ambuja ma in to the emergency ward...and there was none in the hospital with a security who was dosed off...

"Hello, hello" here is an emergency please call the duty doctor to help!!! Ambuja is pregnant, and she will need immediate help.

Uh...uh.as the security woke up and he said

"Amma...these duty doctors sometime they come, but mostly they are busy in visiting hospitals in town and cities as they pay them well." Oh my God. We are paying for the Doctors as we form the Governments as Mary yelled at the security.

"Hold on. I will call the chief."
"Dr. There is a patient who is in emergency' Can you come here soon..?"
"Velu, I live here in town, and it will take at least 1 hour to reach up there. Ask the Nurse to administer emergency care."

As Venu hangs up the phone....Ambuja was unconscious.

"Amma. Ambuja...please look...look...you will be fine."

The chief Nurse administers some medications after checking her pulse rate. The pulse rate is dropping...let me take her to the emergency ward. This could be a syserian case which I cannot help... need the chief to be here. After a while the Chief had arrived. And there was no pulse rate at all. "Dr. what happened?" we asked anxiously, after a long wait.

"She is dead" I am sorry…as he wrote off any chances of revival. It was just another patient for the Chief. The only mother of a two children is dead for lack of medical help on-time. The next morning was a Panchayat lead who had claimed so many reasons of the lack of responsiveness so on and so forth as it happens every year as part of the regular panchayat meetings. My father and I were there in the meetings, as a kid I raised a question:

"Sir. Why did you kill the mother?"

"Damn it. What did you say?" I did not kill anyone. My dad is a modest person, who did not want me in troubles, as he said. Kris. Just be quiet. We cannot change the world. "No papa. I will change my surroundings as much as possible."

The above incident was deeply rooted in my conscious and I was looking for answers within during my high school talking to my friends about the basic needs of humans; Though, I was a carefree boy, I did well in studies and asked questions to my friends and teachers who had answers to most of it.
In my history class.

"Sir. It is great to heart the glory of India in the past. How can we regain in the future?" Well. Good question. The reason is a good governance practices in those days with ministers and local administrators for every 1000 people and the visits of the king helped in taking care of individuals"

I had thought about this…and the death of Ambuja which was haunting me, even in my dreams. In that night, I had a dream where Ambuja was crying for help…

"Appo, Nee thangachiya paathu kiviya paa;"
("which means you would take care of my younger daughter right?"
As my tears started rolling down…and my mom asked me. "What happened to you?"

"Mom. Nothing I am fine."

"Just sleep well da." As she patted me on my shoulders to get some rest. There is nothing we could do! As I continued with my studies and busy in exams as usual with the cricket was my passion of those days. First a small village hospital has started operational, with a doctor in attendance every day and specialists from Tiruchi visiting once a month. The next was a non-formal learning center, which incorporates traditional knowledge in farming and watershed management and weaving in its curriculum while meeting the minimum level of learning prescribed by NCERT. A data entry center, which gives exposure to rural youth to computers, while providing them a source of income has also been opened in a seven-acre extent of land donated by KRISH's uncle Sethuraman. With some difficulty, he has obtained broadband facility for the center.

"When I looked at the transformation of villages in last two to three decades in Kannur, and many more villages. There were no major changes, as I have noticed"

He dreamt about it since his school days to work for a decade to fulfill his personal financial commitments before venturing in to the social activities. It was not easy in the beginning after returning from the US. There was a phase of close to a year with several questions from the localities with a raise bro's of whether World Community would sustain, or perhaps World Community has the ability to transform. The financial commitment is huge; I had been using all the finances that I earned from the US for the initial hospital. I request each of you to donate denominations of Rs.100/ to support each of these children,

Like a flow of river and the message of a Mahatma with his unique views. Perhaps if you realize the sufferings around, you must create an impact to visualize. There is a lot that you can teach by expending two hours a month, or a business plant and many things in small steps for instance a Doctor who can help part time

"Arise, Awake and STOPNOT Till the Goal is reached"
>   -   Swami Vivekananda

I was about fifteen years when I was studying in High School in Trichy…It happened

"Dear Students, hurry up, we have called your parents. Our school will remain shut for next couple of days due to an emergency. You all can go home now…" as my class teacher who always takes care of notes and the timeline was in a hurry to go back home, followed by a short announcement from the Headmaster. Reverad.Father. Tambaku. Students there is a serious problem outside, stay together as we would drop each of you back home;

In the Gandhi road, there were barricades and Police force with gunmen and watershed and teargas to find some men carrying weapons were arrested…as I pass through the street, a trajectory of stone hit my forehead…perhaps it looked like a perfect situation…

"Amma, Amma" as I felt through the pain and I started crying; the care take, Mohan had immediately held with his handkerchief and asked me to be seated I didn't know what happened for almost 45 mins there were many military vehicles, and our bus was stopped for more than half an hour. What is going on? As I asked….

There is a communal rage. If someone ask you about your caste. Say that you are a Christian!!! And tell your name as Vincent. As the advice came in from my senior…rightly said there were few men looking for more to cremate as we were haunted by the dreadful eyes and wanting to massacre people for no reason at all. The incident had left me in a state for almost a week till the life was back to normal with the loss of men, women and children mounting up to hundred as indicated in the newspaper.

"Appa (Dad)…anything that we can do to change that?"

"Of course, you can. When you become an adult and a good politician to teach people about the results of what they are doing to their children. Now, It is your homework and higher education." as he indicated his plans for me for the future.

"Ok daddy." As I gasped through the window.

My house in Trichy was a beautiful one with a back yard for cows where my maid milks the cow in the morning, a pair of pigeon that I feed in the morning. The cooing cocks are brave enough over the roof top. My dad and I take care of the garden filled with roses, hibiscus, and some medicinal herbs that my dad had planted; especially I could remember the scent of the eucalyptus plant whenever I helped my dad in the garden, and my siblings were modest without many fights when I grew up, Indeed they taught me in maths, and science to excel them in both these subjects as I exclaim.

The house is one of the ancestral properties, with the large pillars supporting the ceiling, and the central space for rain water harvesting… (muttram) as we call!!! The hall was very spacious with 'unjal' that can host at least four to five, in those days I spent mostly in the Unjal whenever I am back from the school to my sister's envy. The traditional house had simple architecture with the basics of ample air and light circulation everywhere…as I realized the offices cov-

ered with glass and you gaze the clouds like a pris-
oners.

I looked back as a stranger with the build modest
huts which are really comfortable than the contemporary brick and mortar houses as I could smell the
ground and the warmth of the bamboo pillars
around. It was simple to withstand rain, and sun.
With required window panels of large French archi-
tect with glasses designed by children, the so called
impoverished fingers have painted beautiful pictures
of what they felt and loved in hills, and rivers.

My home for next couple of days was well lit with an
oil lamp was just amazing with no pollution to the
environment. Which itself is a social service in my
view…and the poor children were around playing
happily and the master arrives…KRISH there was a
pin drop silence, as they love him so much and let
him talk. I exclaimed within myself. How may I
wonder a thousand families are dependent with over
five years of day/and night of Kris efforts are just
imminent. It portrays a beautiful picture of his self
and image grown larger in over a thousand household. He has not done anything for any reason or
gain or even without any anticipation.

Each of these children calls him by 'Anna, Yenga
Vooru Shivaji' The warrior of my village, and they
think this man has hailed from the heavens. Now, I
have become one among these children with a similar
thought of this man from the heavens. Perhaps a
messenger of Kannur village, and I wish him extend

his wings to every part of the world where human consciousness strives hard to survive...and I wish and pray to God to give him enough wealth and power to accomplish what he is desiring for the future generations

'Pasangla. Homework panniteengala...Did you do your homework?' Yes sir. And No sir from a few back bench crew members. After completing the sessions for an hour and a half, he picked up a chat with those adolescent kids for keeping their focus.

I enjoyed playing with children and the reason for some smiles...with the songs of Bharathiyar!

Jaathi ellaiyadi papa
Kula thaazchi vuyarchi sollal paavam'

"There is not any lower or upper caste,
My dear children....remember discriminating
Someone by caste/birth is a sin."

Thus, infusing the idealism through the young minds shaping clays in to diamonds and I am sure each of these children of the future generations would sprout as a true citizen of this country.

"Pasangla. You need to stay, three of you. Thalamuthu, Hari and Sebi follow me. He takes them to his home to teach them simple breathing practices called 'Nadhi Suddhi' a profound technique for concentration by streamlining breathing..."

After a year, I hear from them. Especially Thal-amuthu has passed with over 80% in the 10TH GRADE was just amazing as I felt it was way beyond any expectations. Indeed KRIS has won a battle by improving % passes in almost seven schools and there are many schools which are in the list of WORLD COMMUNITY to empower children and encourage.'

When I was visiting the neighboring villages, I had found so many Kinder Garden children were mal-nourished. Indeed, I found one of them falling down in the prayer sessions out of extreme heat. I just ex-amined with a town hospital doctor, who had con-firmed her for the malnutrition...while some of the kids in the country are obese. There were close to over an hundred children those who are malnour-ished...Immediately the day after, I thought about a program plan with the decisive approach to solve a problem in the resolution plane of my mind in the astute way of solving problems.

"Team, Let us build a Nutrition Plan." as I had typed a few points in my laptop to build a plan for the fu-ture. Today, the program is operational with more than hundred children in various schools and num-ber of projects is ever increasing. The inspection letter from the chief and Dr. Tom who had audited several health care centers around the world has some re-marks on the progress. I did not want to settle for anything small and the letter as I hold read this...highlighting all my challenges.

I used the risk mitigation plan of back up resources based on anticipated risks as IBM had taught me the principles of managing risks…Our education is not a waste as it helped often to make right decisions.

Gene picked up a volunteer in World Community a young man named 'Muthu'…

Gene: "Muthu, what do you do with the World Community organization..?"

M: "Sir, I belong to the World Community."

"What do you mean?"

"This is my country and Kris is my mother & father!"

"Can you explain a little bit about the way you got into the World Community organization…?"

M: "Well Buddy! I would like to know your background."

"It was my childhood, everything my father and my neighbors, friends and God did not intend to set it right until the day I met Kris sir."

"Hold on. Indeed, God has sent you Kris?" she interrupted.

"Yes. Ok. God has finally opened his eyes!"

"No…No…Indeed. You have opened your heart!"

"Okay. Okay."

"I was convicted and sent to Jail for three months due to consuming illicit liquor, during this time my mom and sister were taken care by World Community and thanks to KRIS who had counseled me. Not just by asking me to be good, by showing me the way to be good through services... I realized it when my mom was in the brink of committing suicide..."

"Sami (God) mare vanthu kapathitaru!!!
(Like a savior he came and saved us!)
"He saved me and my family. I don't have words of my gratitude...as he spoke with tears rolling down."

Ok ok...well done my friend as I spoke to him...with KRIS looking clearer than ever with his gleaming eyes of confidence with absolute integrity, and humbleness. Here is it ....despite all the hardships, the first health care center. And I am determined doing it in every single village in India and anywhere in the world, as every human being is entitled for the basic benefits. If the respective Governments don't do it, I will do it for the people of the world and for every global citizen.

World Community had been founded in January 2005 with the mandate to empower rural India to transform itself into a socially stimulating, self-reliant and growth oriented community. World Community's project in Kannur, Near Trichy, is the Organizations first attempt to exercise the idea of holistic rural development?

To which end, World Community has set up a health center, a school, and vocational and agricultural Training programs, among other endeavors, With the vision of transforming Panchayat schools. As per the plan, I integrated all these elementary and high schools with over one thousand children with proper teachers from the neighboring schools.

Some of these teachers those who are part of the World Community organization are interacting closely with the Parents in the Parent-Teachers association, there were challenges in terms facing the anticipation of parents as we are educating every household in terms of encouraging them for higher studies. As a development plan, we have educated parents in the annual meeting, I've emphasized on empowering students with proper high-school education. The entire infrastructure for the schools and education for a year was funded from my savings earned from the US.

Early our expenses for seven schools and five health care, Tele-medicine centers with panchayat development centers. The Asha foundations in the US, formed by the Indian born citizens are funding up to 3-4 lakhs for the education. The free break-fast programme and the children with disorders during the survey with required nutrition supplement include our financials.

There have been several questions from the localities in the villages, perhaps criticisms which are common and I hope and believe these people would eventually understand the funding. The future plan for the World Community organization is to streamline Panchayat Governance to empower every village. The collector, MLA's are not anywhere closer to the villages, World Community's responsibility is to empower Panchayat in order to benefit every village.

I feel it is extremely important to create jobs for every adult in the villages, by providing skills. As a next step, I would like to stop addictions. I fear the consequences of alcohol consumption in the villages, especially in the adolescents and adults with affecting their personal health, family and the financial burden resulting in many deaths in the society. My goal is completely plan for the eradication of controlling addictions by provides counseling.

My vision is to strive for good quality education for each of these children who should be able to work in any part of the world. I have observed many top performers in recent times with a little push and interest inculcated. As Swami Vivekananda opined...My real intent is to help them achieve basic needs through enough skills and basic education, and further expanding their consciousness by research and self-inquiry.

Also, give it back to the community by supporting each other anywhere in the world. I am teaching these children to support humanity. It really does not matter whether it is in India or Africa…the one who is able to create smiles around by alleviating the pains of others is the one who has done the job.

On the other day. I had a dream, When God was enquiring with Chitra Gupta: About the good and bad deeds. There was a man who was caught for his bad deeds and God asked.

God: Mani. "You are a politician. Why didn't you help others as you had the opportunity?"

Mani: "I was good. Until the system changed me;"

"Well. You have excuses. Ok. Spend some time in the community center of the heaven and then transition to heaven." As God opined.

The other man was bewildered as he cried.

"Oh my Lord. Father, pardon my sins;"

"My son. You are a Christian father. Why you have so many criminal case registered."

"It is all a plan to malign my name as the father said…then why didn't you allow me when I was there in the church."

"Well. Father. You were interrupting my business;"

"Why didn't you show me to the world?" asked God.

"Because you were interrupting my fame!!!" replied the Christian father.

Finally, God ordered him to be thrown to hell for misguiding men and women...This is how life continues as we are misguided and tend to misguide. As much as possible, you should be ready to help others as it brings you good deeds. The more you sow good deeds, more you would reap as the cause and effects theory. It cannot be other way!!!

Your sufferings have a reason and the social setup is the cause of all poverty in the world. God created humans or perhaps it was his manifestations as Vedanta says and you are part of it. If it is so. It was due to the greedy politicians, and a few religious leaders that you have lost the faith in god and the ability to reconnect yourself to the eternal being. You have it undiscovered as Buddha says! India, my land from time immemorial has never invaded against countries, as its primary goal was reaching the peak of the consciousness through self-inquiry and reasoning.

Hence, many emperors have come out of their kingdom in search of truth. Siddhartha the Buddha is an example and many more that followed his footsteps. The Epics of Hinduism teaches you virtues of personalities such as Rama, and Krishna who had been revelations or avatars of God as mythology claims to induce some good behavior in each of you

We were able to connect wirelessly to the rest of the world with the vision of APJ's technology come true.

Our broad band connection is the back bone for our Software development, E-learning initiative and Tele-Medicine – each one of them making a huge difference to our efforts here. In the first place, this type of connection to a rural area beyond the normal limits, it was a tremendous effort by the local staff of BSNL.

Lately, for the past 3 months, we have been having constant issues with this connection. And I don't think the initial level of efforts is there now to try solving the issues. Normally, such issues are not one-dimensional but our working culture wants to solve that way. In this case – distance from sender tower to us is larger than normal limits.

I think, in solving issues that has a high amount of Social impact, one needs to first decongest the small bottle necks. While, a larger and permanent solution could come from the "one-dimensional" issue – the high level of technicalities, economics and time for creating such solutions means insisting on it can tremendously slow social progress.

When coming back, she visited Amutha whose husband moved out of her life immediately after a boy was born. Amutha has very few relatives and her son is also not a healthy boy. While she goes out to do daily labor work, she is not the "strong" ones whom a farm owner/employer prefers...she can't be a load (WO) man, masons won't prefer her or she can't do paddy thrashing. She won't get work all days because of this and she may not be equally paid like the rest. Now, through a Government housing scheme she was offered a "pucca concrete" house for her thatched home.

The Government pays Rs.70, 000, part of it by supplies. Like many of the ill planned schemes, some 3 lakh homes were to come in the 1st year across the state.

The timing was wrong, demand shot up; prices of raw materials went up by nearly 200%. A brick which was costing Rs. 2.75 a month before is now Rs.6... and if the person is lucky to get a hand on it. Anyway, lot of her neighbors convinced Amutha to go for it. Now, she is caught between the devil and the deep blue sea, with her house raced down and not knowing how to finish this building!

Amutha found a patient ear in Preeti to tell all her life sorrows and sufferings. She being pushed into a dependent life all through her life and the daily suffering she has to go through, any Tom, Dick and Harry has an idea for her.

I have seen many times she takes a decision which hurts her later. We can endlessly debate on the attitude change that change makers have to bring in her...but for someone who suffers day in and day out... who is loved by very few, who goes empty stomach many days, on whom the society slants its concocted eye ... the only comfort given is love and sharing.

Looking at the aged farmers. A deep thought intruding me...How can one ever expect a man chasing greedy goals to understand what it means for a farmer when the rains disappoint him yet again? Or how it shatters a villager to see arable lands without cultivation?

How can one expect a man who spends half his life in an AC chamber to understand what if feels like to stand on a parched land feeling the sun's fury on one's head and to look into a well that shows no traces of water despite the numerous bores that scar it?

How can one ever get a man, skipping a job that pays him in lakhs for another that pays him a few thousands more, to understand how folks in the village work on all the days of the week for much longer hours and do far more strenuous work for an annual income that amounts only to those few thousands?

I believe cultivation is tough job. Constant and persistent vigilance, sheer hard work, endless perseverance is what it takes to get a good yield. In the end their crop is sold at a mere amount. So, what lies ahead for the farmers there if they don't move out and the current state of affairs don't improve? Can we hold them responsible for wanting a better standard of life that their endless efforts in their farms don't seem to accommodate?

What destiny awaits these fertile lands when each farmer decides to move into towns in pursuit of better pay and a better quality of life? How do we propose to feed the huge population if such a thing ever happens?

Folks in the villages seem quite ignorant of how life in the towns is. But their ignorance seems much lesser than the ignorance town folks have about village life.

People in the cities have no clue how a village functions, and how dramatically their way of life is changing the rural life. Media seems to be barely reaching out to addressing certain issues they must have addressed ages ago.

Issues that deserve all the attention they can afford to get; issues that would certainly hold much more relevance to the Indian masses than certain other news pieces that cram our media like which business tycoon is dating which actress.

With all misplaced priorities and misplaced focus are commonplace problems. Sometimes they don't make much difference. At other times, they make all the difference there is to make. Sad.

For the refreshing company they offered me, the endless chats we shared, for the visits they accompanied me on, for all their time and patience with me, I thank Saroja and Karthi. I learnt more about art from them than I could ever hope to teach them.

For those sweaty mornings we spent working together on cataloging, her sweet way of humming

while we were at it, I shall remember Then. I hope the kids still adore her like they did when I was there, and I hope they don't test her patience as much!
For all those fresh conversations laced with a rustic wit, for all the profound knowledge about various fields that he imparted to me, I shall remember Ponnudurai Sir. I hope his daughter, Ahalya, is doing fine and that his wife's scanning has shown good results...

For all those evenings that I spent running behind her, I shall remember my first ever cycle student... I hope Mallika is doing well. Tell her I want my ride with her, as a pillion, on her cycle the next time I visit!

For those evenings that we spent scraping the violin, the guffaws we shared about extinct species, the little nothings in our evenings, the delicious parting lunch that she and her mum prepared for us, the pleasant and patient, the haunting trademark smile of hers, I shall remember Mythili. I hope this multi-faceted lady has been practicing sketching. Have you, Mythili? To all those refreshing coffees that she took special efforts to brew just for me, to all those mouthwatering dishes she indulged me with, to all the motherly love and affection that she gave me...

I shall forever remain indebted to Jayamma. I hope she has learnt to sign her name right now. Somebody please tell her I miss the coffees' she used to brew me in the kitchen, after freshly cleaning the place with cow-dung-mixed-water! To those endless engaging conversations that captured my days effortlessly, to all those narration filled evenings that seemed ever too short for me to let go, to all the borrowed eccentricities.

I can add to my own character henceforth, to all those enthusiastic pursuits that he set me unto, to all the glorious moments that he managed to spare for me despite his time being too expensive to be spent on trifles like me, to have taught me just about every lesson that I have learnt during my stay there and for opening my vision to capture new perspectives of life that I had never seen existing before... to all of these and much more.

I can barely thank Senthil enough. He is 'THE' magic charm behind World Community ... the wonderful man who can ceaselessly manage to keep you in awe of him!

Besides, Sir's daughter is doing well. Manohar Sir, I hope he is not as busy as Kris usually keeps him! Gajendran Sir, I hope he has been hunting as much as he likes. I hope Soubhagyam Ma'am and Selvaraj Si-rare keeping well... And, how are the folks in the Chutti school and the BPO? I can only wish they're all keeping well... and that I shall!

Finally, without realizing the plans of the Divine Nature...I fell in love with Preeti who supported in various projects. My marriage was made in heaven as I had no intentions of getting married at any point of my career, happening at the same place that brought Preeti and me together as also many of us.

Who knows what the Divine plans are for each of us. I tied the knot of oat into a Divine relationship. Where the man has pronounced a woman as his wife...to support her and praise her for what she his. As an embodiment of the Divine Nature...

"Gene was a little depressed for a while as she shook her hands bidding 'Good Bye' with her gentle hug...before she decided to venture in to teaching 'Political Science' in Harvard Business school , which had left an everlasting remark in my heart!

Who else would know the angry communities united in my marriage with Preeti, and how would Gene understand the communal clashes as my memories flashing across about my marriage, and the innocuous Preeti seeking my smiles every day!!!

I decided to go with life without forcing anything to happen as Nature had its final cast in everything from the smallest of events to the significant events.

*

I met Aparna who was selected as part of an NGO. Volunteer Programme in 2010, an information science and engineering student from Bangalore, as one of the candidates who got through the initial scanning process. After many weeks of eager waiting, I finally found myself aboard the train to Trichy - all set to spend a month volunteering with World Community Trust.

A beautiful young woman from Bangalore who had visited us in the year 2010
Gene: 'Aparna, How do you find this place? You do not have an AC? And a nice car that you drive back in Bangalore'

"Oh no...I am enjoying my time out here with the morning birds and the alliance with Nature working in the field gives me some exercise; perhaps, this is what I have been looking for long...World Community has made an impact in my life as it did with several thousands of families around as I see during the Aid season in 2010 about my first day gave me sufficient hints about how the rest of my stay there would be like. To the unmatched, unsurpassed hospitality that I was smothered with, the selfless ability of the folks there to adapt to anybody and make people feel like they have always belonged there.

To all those wonderful people who have touched my life in ways that I cannot forget, to all the memories that I have managed to capture from these few days and to everything that has changed about me since my visit here, I shall forever remain indebted to World Community!!!

Kris is a man who has connected technology to the villages, riding a bicycle carrying a laptop wired to the rest of the world, who has put the village of Kannur to the rest of the world. I hear that every time "Technology is a means to help you all;" Is it so.as the multimillion dollar projects have not succeeded to the extent of food for all? The caveat is that only a limited few have managed to find projects and it continue with the link of upper middle classes, probably to some extent middle classes have prospered by the technology, however the plight of the villages remain the same.

KRIS demonstrated that 'leadership' – Leading by example from the front with the technology power points, engineering in wireless technology and civil engineering by constructing low cost houses for the villagers…and contemporary farming techniques. And many more as the projects list almost extend every year as the projects started with education to the computer technology for the poor with more than ten desktops installed in the lab.

It is not just feeding the poor. Indeed it is a broader vision of empowering each one of them…in to leaders of tomorrow with the cancer awareness programs…welfare of the women program etc. and the list is extending beyond. Education, Health care and computers!!!! With the skill development program to help youth from addictions to the skillful resources. And the women to just the household stuff to the technology and communication.

A local villager could speak little bit of English. A local village kid asked:

"How are you sir?"

"I am fine thank you" as I replied

"Pleasure is mine…as it came crisp with the tender hands offering me a tender coconut with love."

"What's your name girl? Sir, my name is Veena…" Veena is an intelligent girl with her father was affected with HIV, who was admitted at the hospital. When the entire community did not support Veena, and her mom…

Kris did support wholeheartedly to save the child from the mental torture. She is just fine, above all she is our child my friends as he spoke aloud to the meeting, reminding me of the freedom fighter V.O.Chidambaram Pillai of pre-Independence days. She is our child pa….let's take care as he walked adding another one to the World Community.

I was constantly reminded by the ideals of Swami Vivekanda, Mahatma Gandhi and Buddha. The ideals of truth, and compassion, have helped me in forging the ideals of World Community. While Vivekananda was driven by the ideology of changes inner, the conducive environment is required with the basic needs to be fulfilled, hence, I decided to start at the grass roots of humanity to empower communities as my observation is that basic needs to be fulfilled as a priority;

Perhaps a similar revolution is required, and this time it is not against anyone, it is to join hands with each of you to form the one-hand Governance to support each other in the journey of consciousness;

As a primary factor, our wealth is not distributed. In the 18th century, Karl Marx was instrumental in forming the principles of socialism, where in a real democracy each of your basic needs taken care in a democratic Nation.

I have witnessed it in the United States, which has every reason to be the best country in the world with robust Governance. The Eastern countries such as India has intelligence, however the democracy seem to have taken a back seat with a few corrupt politicians and lack of Governance to be able to implement measures to support individuals, resulting in funds not reaching the individuals for the welfare of humanity.

I feel in a similar context, most part of Africa despite Natural resources, seems to have gone below the level of poverty with malnutrition children dying out of hunger every year. One of my visions is to extend the model of micro-economy to every village in the world to support these communities in their growth and self-reliance.

It is your birth right to claim fulfillment of basic needs, if a Government is unable to provide it. It is a definite failure of democracy. World Community envisages the transformation of Indian villages into a socially stimulating, self-reliant, growth oriented community rooted in the principles of Truth - a society where people practice and interact with the highest moral values. The belief that every human-being deserves a good quality of life is the driving force of the World Community Ashram - a rural empowerment facilitation center, henceforth termed as World Community.

We will work in rural villages of India to create an atmosphere where people have the space to practice truth. We will lead, create opportunities, facilitate and mentor. We will take a holistic development approach touching all aspects of the society - be it local economy and revenue, social needs like health; education; sanitation; infrastructure, civic and panchayat systems and also spiritual needs.

We will not only understand and facilitate work for the identified needs of the current society but more importantly lead with a foresight into the future growth of the society. Through the entire process, we will partner with the local populace and nurture leaders among them for eventual take over.

We believe in the realization of the fundamentals of Panchayat Raj as envisaged by Gandhi. Any community should be able to own the ideas that are needed for their continuous development — be it their physical, civic or spiritual. Owning of the ideas means collectively create new thoughts and create/manage resources to implement and execute it.

At the individual level, each individual should be able to self-realize his/her own potentials, without any distinction based upon caste or creed. This would in essence mean to build an environment where even the most ordinary person lives with self-respect

When I enquired about the plans for the future, it was even more astounding…as KRISH's contemporary plans for the future taking the world beyond:

I am intending to provide a conducive environment for children, women and adults. A robust governance of Panchayat to implement with transparency in spending in every phase of the project implementation. The micro economy is concerned with how supply and demand interact in individual markets for goods and services.

Did you ever think about the unfair, uneven economics? And the inequality in someone in the cities making money vs. relatively a poor farmer who works harder through the day;

I did not want to interrupt as the theories of Karl Marx were imminent from the modest person of Kannur in a dhoti, portraying the principles of Gandhism.

Jay: Well Kris. '*What is the pragmatic approach?*'

The pragmatic approach is to analyze the current economic reforms and by empowering village panchayats and enabling more transparency can elevate the communities in villages. Next most important point is to provide enough funding's to help them self-sustain without too much of dependencies.

The basics of good education, schools and infrastructure and inter-connectivity to the villages are a must like in the United States. This would create more jobs and rapid migration of students to other cities and deploy contemporary farming techniques to boost productivity!

There is a lot more …

Ok. As I interrupted Kris for a while for a short break to complete the hot servings of cookies with a nice cup of brewed coffee reminding our stay in the United States. As Kris continued non-stop with the future plans with a plan chalked out in the board.

The finances was a concern as the organization is primarily funded by friends and some well-wishers which is not going to sustain the growth of the community with the ever increasing needs of projects and funding needs by the way of corporate funding or the Government project funding. Either way we are ready to partner with the major corporates in adopting villages as we have 700,000 thousand villages it will need stupendous efforts in next few decades to transform

Finally, if you ever need India to be a great Nation in the world arena, villages have to be empowered and self-reliant. The vision of World Community for 2020 is to cover villages in south and north-east with the recent disaster of Uttarkhand is inflicting pain in my heart for the welfare of people in the North eastern part of India.

Beyond 2020 if Divine Nature wants us beyond the shores, I am prepared and I will be able to take World Community to several million households in the African continent. Swami Vivekananda was trying to change the fate of poverty in India by educating the masses through the spiritual empowerment *Give me hundred men; I will change the World!!!*

As I thought; it is deeply saddening to see the psychological maturity of a few who intervene and interrogate the motto of organizations which are contemporary with small Panchayat's challenging the vision of World Community.

But Kris was relentless in his goals, despite the discouraging words of some of the localities to the Government officials, he continued with available funds and the overseas connections through friends and families extending his Bangalore chapter of World Community rolled out in the year 2010.

All good things will expand; no matter how much opposition exist, as Nature will continue to exercise her will. It was a perfect cast of the Mother Nature in her gracious eyes opened towards ignorant villagers. Though, if you do not support; perhaps you should refrain from hurting the vision, and goals.

In spite of all these challenges, Kris is working toward the common goal of empowering villages and the rest all is secondary. From the circle of social community expanding through the media such as Facebook, across the shores of India and overseas in connections with Asha foundation of the United States. Each village should be made self-reliant with less or no dependencies, let the cities ride on the villages and not the other way. The native swadeshi products should compete in global standards with required subsidies and every MNC organization must be resorting to adapting a village for a certain tax-rebate, which would be entitled.

If someone is working abroad, the following family should pay FT. Foreign Trade tax or foreign work tax which would go to the village budget for the development of required infrastructure in the villages. Thus, it can be balanced and further by the way of sharing work with the software organizations extending its secondary arms in the towns, funded and supported by the governmental organization is a must to-do activity to sustain the rural empowerment policies.

Let these good rules be established as amendments to the constitution and every citizen of this country should be eligible for the social security fund to sustain mounting economic issues and reforms. The roots of wisdom is expanding, thus driving all ignorance in the mankind to strive for joining hands for creating a community where women, and children are safe with the basic needs fulfilled in every villages; above all a tribute to Mahatma Gandhi.

For this gentle man in his ardent style of body, mind and spirit dedicated to the welfare of people and a great community which was in the brink of absolute destruction. The classical Shivaji the warrior has arrived in the village of Kannur, a Chola kingdom once is now the onus of draught weather conditions. I hope the Chola warrior can take the village of Kannur with the emerging Doctors, Scientists and Engineers.

A silent revolution has just begun!!!!
A silent revolution has just begun!!!!

Oh my dear brothers, and sisters, open your eyes and ears of wisdom with heart filled in love to support humanity to strive in success in empowering villages. Let's join hands to support this great organization and the vision of World Community is every Indian's dream.

Often times it reminded me of Mr. Thomson and his rules and messages to carry forward, which later changed my life forever. These incidences were fresh in my memory, as though it happened a few minutes ago;

"I had been determined to campaign for the Panchayat elections to support over a thousand families to expand the mode to all neighboring villages…"

"Anna…Neenga election la nikkanoom to help more number of people" as the villages said unanimously. Therefore, I registered my name for the Panchayat elections. It was early in the morning…as I usually wake up at four in the morning for my prayers and planning the work for the day. There were three men with masks who lit fire in the Organic farm. And they sent an intimidating courier with a message to stop contesting as my interest grew larger to contest…

After intense campaign, the results were not in my favor. I was rather thinking more about people's expectations as you cannot assume anything. However, Thuraisammy and his friends of my school indicated something went on at the electorate which they cited few lakhs spent by the opposition party. I related this to the former incidence to find there could be something fishy…I didn't want any unpleasant issues amidst good things and progress with WORLD COMMUNITY as I continued with my reforms with my own sources. But the above incidents have kept me vibrating in my mind. Why would someone disrupt in humanity services and the answer was the animal instincts in humans have not been resolved yet which is a constant conflict in most of them, resorting to measures of crime; with a vow of not to identify these young men whom I have identified!

As I opened the scribbling in the package in Tamil. It was written with some grammatical errors which gave me a clue of who had done this…I want to teach you a lesson for your election campaign was written in the local language…

"Vungalluku oru pahdam katho tharuveyan…(I will teach you a lesson)" Instead it was written as 'padam' which is a frequent error as I traced back in all seven schools to find a similar age group of students who are making these mistakes.

"Ayyah. Can you identify who has similar mistakes." as the teachers had convened to confess on how many of these students are making such mistakes? Kris narrowed down a few, and finally a group of three men from the same school 'Pennadam Hsc.' ok. He called these men…he knew them by eyes as they were struggling to stand in front of his piercing eyes.

Like a lion he stood in front of them…Pasangala, what did you do? "Saar, naanga yedhuvum seyala…" What?

"Is it so…where is your sister in the hospital for treatment. Just think what has helped her my son…"

"Saar. My sister's operation is fine because of your hospital and my mom is happy as my sis has re-gained her vision…"

Durai "You don't know how much we funded for the operation" it came from all the hard work of one week efforts which yielded only ten thousand which I kept to pay the salary for all our employees. Now, that I paid for your sis' operation. With no money in hand…what am I doing?

Saar 'yenna manichidonga saar' (I am so sorry) with rolling tears in his cheeks...

"Yampa…Yampa why are you doing this?"

"Saar. Pannayar yennaku ayiram roobai ko-dutharoo.(The village head had bribed me)" The rich man in town bribed me Rs.1000 one thousand rupees to destroy the farm! And others joined him and fell under my feet. as a token of reverence and sorry state What am I doing? It seemed like the whole World was against me!

At first I lost the elections, and second I could not save a yearlong efforts going waste in the farm over-night…and the cattle are all infected by virus. As I stood up to let me emotions go…with the open skies and dry farm land and failed agriculture with my dhoti finding its solace on the ground feeling its warmth. Just let it go. Today was not yours but to-morrow will be yours. Just get up and do your deed!!!!

The resounding truths with a copy of Bhagwat Geetha talking to me who I have not read through for months as I bought it from the book store in Trichy…

> *"Do your duty*
> *I will yield as results"*
> -   *Bhagvad Gita*

The above statement as uttered by Krishna…to Arjun ahead of the deadly war of Gurushethra...

Arjun laments: "Oh mighty Krishna, I find my neph-
ews, my cousins and brothers in front of me…how
can I find courage to find against them as my heart is
melting away in love?"

"Arjuna, It is not you who ride as I do and it is all my
manifestations. Each of them is part of me including
you and there is no one who is away from me; *Just do
your duty, as I'd yield as results;"*

I have read through the duty consciousness and
Swami Vivekananda's speech in Chicago was significant addressing the entire group of professionals as
'Brothers and Sisters' the entire group listened to the
next one hour where he walked them through the
core principles of Vedanta. And the part is God's
manifestations in the universal brotherhood as he
concluded the speech with a foray of love and affection from the fellow beings in the United States, the
land of opportunities. I just reflected on these state-
ments. My failures were too little and too insignifi-
cant as I decided to plan for seeking more sponsor-
ship…On that day, I wrote a memorandum:

My dear friends and families, I strive hard for success
to help every villager success. As Mahatma said every village should be empowered, and every child
should deserve the best of the education. World
Community has foundation pillars of education, jobs
for adults, women empowerment and spiritual
growth as a holistic plan for each individual across
the Globe. I decided not to ask for sponsors. If you do

will for something to support for a cause. Of course you can. Contact me Kris...as I signed the letter and send it to many people whom I know'

The first response was from a foundation called 'Asha' which his predominantly started by the elite group of men and women from India, those who have settled in the United States. The response was overwhelming with over a hundred response with intense care and love from overseas through the job connections, and my school connection which had fetched some money to survive and repair the damage caused in the Organic farm and treat the cattle:

The mother as I call her...cattle was just lying down with high fever and in India; It is a sign of ominous and a bad omen to let the cow die. As I called off for a vet. He injected and gave some medications. "Lakshmi ma." As I called her 'Lakshmi ma...opens your eyes as she was suffering from high temperature and I called the vet once again. The vet hospital finally sent a young nurse to administer some injections to the cow and take care...

Nila her name in twenties working as a nurse in the vet clinic. She was passionate and beautiful with brown eyes for her age of impeccable rigor!!!
"Sar. What is the problem for her? As she passionately touched the Lakshmi ma. She is sick and has very high temperature."

"No problem saar. I have treated many Lakshmi's in her smile." As she smiles at me.

"Okay, then treat her now and take care of her for next couple of days. Where do I stay…?"

"Here near the cow dung as Lakshmi ma will need you anytime. Just keep an eye on her."

"Saar…there is a lot of mosquitos."
"Okay. Don't cry. You can rest there in my room. I will wake up if Lakshmi ma needs you. Okay."

The next morning. "Nila, Nila, the sun is up for a long time. Why are you Nila (moon) resting as you promised to save Lakshmi ma (cow)…"
"sorry sar. I was a little tired last night due to travel in last couple of days. Okay.okay"

"Get up and have your breakfast."
Cheese. Just a porridge? She asked with an expression on her face.
"Come on girl, This is kambu koozh and good for health a nutritious drink. Have it and get back to job."
I ordered her about her role.

She was ready in about half an hour and then took charge in her regular attire of a nurse with stethoscope to check the heartbeat of Lakshmi ma…

"Nila, how is she doing?" I asked.
"Sir. She is doing good now, after the first set of medications. Well. I am sorry sir for all that happened!"

"What? I forgot to inject her last night some chloroform to alleviate from pain? "I did that…"

"What saar?" Yes. I had spent few weeks in the cattle farm and I know how to inject and administer medicines. She was touched by his gentleness and not wanting to escalate the matter to the hospital. Lakshmi ma was perfectly fine after a couple of days...

I was reading through the verses of Kamba about Hindu epic Ramayana where he says:

> *She looked down from the balcony,*
> *Where eyes meet of that of Rama;*
> *For a split second of aligned consciousness,*
> *It was a love at the first sight of my consciousness,*
> *Like a rising sun as I felt current wave in myself;*

As I concluded this chapter, I found her ....perhaps the destiny was calling me to find her as I loved Gene wittiness and etiquette of serving the poor. She was on a college vacation, as a project to support the education of poor children...she taught.

"Akka puriyala" (cannot understand!).

She was patient enough to repeat complex math problems and science as she became a full time teacher. She forgets her semester project, apparently as her project became integral part of her life. And my life as well. She is like the women of Bharti...as he claimed.

Born are the women to win

Defy the wisdom of shyness and be bold;
To win hearts of wisdom!

She was a good Opera singer, where my heart finds its solace. Perhaps an angel as I'd recall sent by God to support me in renovating villages with an image of Global picture not by just feeding them, perhaps by bringing out leaders of future generations.

I would like to strive for globalizing food and water as the common and basic needs of humans are same anywhere in the world. Indeed it is the greed that makes it difficult. Nature is by itself democratic as the needs are same, only it varies in quanta based on your relentless desires without boundaries.

As I refer to my archives of my plans…of course most of it has materialized with the interim hard ships: As I read through the The Road map found in my archives during the yester years of 2005-2008….when WORLD COMMUNITY was on paper. The ultimate blueprint for the community services…

My Political Mystery

I have ventured in to politics ever since I was thinking about welfare of the villages. I did not want to shy away from the governance or Panchayat responsibilities. I would like to contest in elections to help the people of my country to bring the change in every villages, unless I have the consistent inflow in the way of charity through the government funds. It will be difficult. I would like to change North Eastern villages of India and beyond the shores of India in every villages in Africa where Gandhi had his foot print.

I would ensure each village would prosper in finally forming one Global Village with seamless integration with cities and towns. Let us share the prosperity as Karl Marx highlighted. It will not be an imposed communism. First time in the history a paradigm shift in socialism blossoming in every part of the world with the common land for all to share.

As we have Nature providing us the same resources to utilize, and why do we create boundaries. I believe every human is very unique and endowed with the eternal consciousness; this would help us understand the basic needs of food, water, which are common needs of every individual. Hence, I would call God is the super Democrat who has planned everyone to share the resources that he has bestowed.

Interrupted by the ring tone of his mobile…'**Vandhe Mataram…Vandhe Mataram**' The irony is that our country men will turn in to unity in a major disaster where the humanity is felt, and the freedom struggles has yielded in tremendous leadership in India.

"Be there one hour at around 7 AM, as the morning at the National High School, Trichy, India. Okay." as my friend Adi advised me. I was not expecting this, as I thought is this a hoax? Someone playing prank…but what followed in a day was a package delivered by the Government of India…The welcome kit announced the award and the formalities. Which will be presented by the president of the country?

Am I going to meet the Chief Minister, which was in my dreams? Is this all real and true as I exclaimed.

"It is real as I insisted on the present events of signifi-cance and reality;"
As my team was awarded for the community ser-vices educating poor children in the neighborhood. There were many cars behold sirens in front of my modest house in Trichy.

The minister walked in to my house.

"Vanakkam Thambi." (morning)

"Niraya seiyareenga." (you do a lot).

Well. I didn't realize the reasons behind the greetings, until the campaign for elections started. He wanted me to support his party to win power at the state, and the center, by campaigning for the Indian Congress.

***

CNN Broadcast Live

8:00 AM EST. NY CNN STUDIO LIVE TELECAST OF
THE CNN HERO-2020

"I am going to introduce you the CNN HERO of the year 2020" as the actor, Sandra bullock in black suit with a beautiful smile up on the stage in the forum filled with the congressman, senate and the actors watching the award ceremony.

"Here you go...The CNN HERO of the YEAR 2020. Today the World Trust empowers villages all over the world in more than fifty Countries, and reaches out to over a TEN million people men, women and children, in over 10,000 villages in India, Africa with its projects profile increasing every year, extending to every part of the world!"

With a firm handshake to Sandra...and Tom hugs him on the stage. Saying 'Hello'

"Gentlemen...put your hands together for the gentlemen...Krish, Mr. Krish a young entrepreneur and a social activist from India"

I was feeling euphoric; with the Hollywood honchos clapping for me...here I am...Krish on the red carpet With the Indian flag hoisted high in the auditorium, as I salute the nation with a pin-drop silence and proceed to the podium.

Ladies and Gentlemen: 'I am Krish, from India and a world citizen as my country has taught me and I thank my spouse, Gita for her support'

With tears rolling...and a bit emotional with Gene who stood by my side. For all these years sharing my project 'The World Community' was indeed a blessing as I thought walking up the ramp!

"Friends, may I ask you to close your eyes and think your children playing with one of these children in Africa, India those who are really poor, and those who are fed perhaps bread or not even that at times. Even today Education, Healthcare is all unaffordable to these masses' what have they done wrong? Is it not a social responsibility for you and me to change a bit?"

It was a minor correction. Not a social service, I did my responsibility and played the part. From Seora Leone to San Francisco the borders are man-made and the God is a Democrat (chuckles). Of course he has provided land, water and air common to each of you, and has endowed you with consciousness. Perhaps we misunderstood the context, and didn't realize the Nature. Each of us are one and the same regardless of the cast, creed, Religion and Nation. Our Nation is the world and we are the citizens of the World!!!

Jai Hind and Thank you USA!!!"

The Nation of grit, determination and a wonderful democracy as I concluded my speech and the path to the world peace has just begun. Indeed a great revolution…is you part of the revolution?

The one who worked with communities in Africa, India empowering villages…here is the video! The video showcased few snippets of the community services in India and Sierra Leone, Africa. The services that I've enabled to help the HIV kids…One of the children who were infected with the deadly virus speaks: "Thanks to Uncle. Who has offered me medicine, and takes care of all of us'.

How many are there? I asked.

Madam…'It's around 100 as the caretaker introduces all other ones' A little girl was one among them that Sandra picked. She hugged her with tears rolling…about 3 years old and the Doctors have informed that she will die in few months looking at her condition'

'But the smiles didn't die as Sandra spoke to the little girl'

"I love you girl. What's your name gal?" asks Sandra. I am Sierra…with a hanky tied around her forehead with the hair tied like a thick bush…and little flowers decorated. 'I like that' pointing at flowers – Sandra…as she lifts her!

Maam…"Ngiyabonga".

Well, Kris next week you have to present the blueprint at the UNESCO…Is that true?

"Of course After that we are flying to the US and then Africa?" I replied.

It was like a dream come true as days passing by allure the future results as I thought.
Gene…Gene…Did you mean it?
Of course. Here is the itinerary as she indicated the baggage that was ready to present all our artifacts to the UNESCO in Paris, France!

It was a revelation as we thought and hugged each other after the presentation at the UNESCO office in the United States and the plan was approved by the Senate to take it further in to Africa with required funding's!!!!

Gene…as I kissed & hugged her…Senate has approved the funding based on the 'The World Community' blueprint…The world community blueprint was missing in the locker. As Kris yelled at each of them...After a while. Gene came in

"I am sorry..." why

I stole the blueprint? For what? I had couriered it to the President's office!

Well. Honey. You have brought in the award and the disaster...you remember few men trying to kill me...these are people who are trying to prevent Senate to award the blueprint for communities as it contains plans to integrated rivers of the world, and one governance...so on and so forth"

Some congressmen didn't want that! Gene...oh my God. I am sorry dear as she hugged Kris:

Here is the brief case "BLUEPRINT CD"
Gene....How did you find the blueprint CD?
Gene..."I picked up the CD from you study room"

'Why did you do that? '

I wanted to send it to the President for the CNN nominations...

Ok...you could have told me? (a little harsh and looking at her). I am sorry Kris....I forwarded it to the CNN Award...

"Alright..." as both hug each other ...

"Mr. President has sanctioned funds in six digits to revive few more villages in Africa"

'Oh My God'. "I am happy" as she exclaims.

Thanks to you my love…as Kris kisses her for her responsibility. My next expedition began to the West coast of Africa….

Epilogue

EXT: 9:00 AM 2022 WEST COAST AFRICA

I was relaxing in the tent of the camping ground

with required wireless and transmitters amidst forest with wild animals; with the only translator and a gun man.

"How do you do Mumbo?" asked a 6.5" ft. tall, strong African man who could fight any adversities and a trustworthy guard who knew the coastal rain-forest in-and out of Cameroon…

"I am fine sir…" lift his that…

After I completed the manuscript deep in the woods; my endeavor extended beyond feeling spirited and helping the communities, as I did venture in the world community service centers to reach out to the remote villages; anywhere in the world and spend some time analyzing their problems, and share the blueprint for a sustainable and self-reliant community to build and help without depending on funds alone.

I moved to the villages in Africa as a vagabond studying Sierra Leone. There were many more poor villages in India. And my venture is to share the blueprint for success in each of the villages and proclaim truth and the basic right of every world citizen. After all, you and I are made of the same stuff. There is no separation from the Divine; it is just an assumption in the mind feeling barricade between you and God.

I woke up the next morning swamped in to the Africa village empowerment planning task discussions with Mumbo Thwart…a guide who could speak a bit of English and guide me as I progress my way…miles away as I felt like a drop in the Ocean.

The courage and the determination of each of you…in supporting the communities

I pledge right here to empower your surrounding communities in whichever way it is possible, wherever you are and whatever you could do to alleviate the sufferings of the world citizens.

"Kris. Here is the orphan child?"

As a beautiful child invited me as a guest on my lap...I just looked in to her eyes...Perhaps the eyes of wisdom with the pains of losing her parents, relatives in the bloody civil war. I cried! Perhaps cried aloud and Mumbo said:

"Sir...Whaz the matter" I just hid my tears as I pretend to pick up my notebook with the program plan starting right away for the welfare of a poor village with rich resources in Africa. With a grit and determination to change the outlook of villages and transforming it conducive to live and work as joyously as ever possible...

Let's take the elephant ride in to the wild forest as I kept searching for answers and 'Nature' is the best teacher that I've ever had, to find the human endeavor as thoughts ceaselessly flowing in and out of my mind...to find the plan...perhaps the blueprint for every village in the world for achieving eternal peace and prosperity.

Papa...as she called 'Sanra. What are you doing here' as Mumbo asked...I am with my papa. As she smiled her way reminding me of the last wish that she had...to travel around the world! I took the elephant ride with Sanra through the rest of my stay in the Sierra Leone…along the West Coast of Africa…

As I am gazing through the beaches and the endless foray of birds, squirrels and the distant hills… someday all the sufferings will end…at some point human envision will be one…and the endeavor of consciousness will evolve.

Papa…"Ngiyabonga" resounding in my heart…though she is gone. Her words are resounding in my heart filled in tears and love for children!!!

Papa…"Ngiyabonga"

As I do hear it from any distant. Perhaps she is not there to hear my words.

"Ngiyakwemukela"

"Ngiyakwemukela"

As more and more children making fun of my poor native African accent…a life time endeavor to continue to gain strength as I think about the other part of the town to support with a memorandum that 'Mumbo' has presented….with the list of To-do's in the morning list.

Publications by the Author

1. *"Anna Heliott" - A Lonely Survivor*
2. *Santa, Me & Tanya!*
3. *Change your Personality in 5 Days*
4. *Success is a Choice – Failure is an Option…*
5. *Heal Thy World (The Seven Golden Rules of Wellness)*
6. *The 7 Golden Rules of ZEN Wisdom*
7. *The Incredible Messiah*
8. *The Ten Affirmations of Truth*
9. *From Sex to Spirituality*
10. *Save the World-ZVM!*
11. *A Silent Revolution*
12. *The Blueprint chip*
13. *The Power of Thought & Inner Engineering*
14. *The Vagabond!*

***

www.ingramcontent.com/pod-product-compliance
Lightning Source LLC
Chambersburg PA
CBHW070356290526
45790CB00004B/1519